NEWPORT
BAY & HARBOUR,
in Pembroke Shire

the late Lewis Morris Esq.

One Mile.

THE ANCIENT BOROUGH OF NEWPORT
IN PEMBROKESHIRE

by
Dillwyn Miles

i

Haverfordwest Library
Dew Street, Haverfordwest
Pembrokeshire, SA61 1SU
Cultural Services Department
Cyngor Sir Dyfed County Council.

First published 1995

ISBN 0-860 750949

Printed by C.I.T. Haverfordwest

CONTENTS

FOREWORD

Historians have passed Newport by, in the main, and those who have made reference to it have not always been kind. Benjamin Heath Malkin, the antiquary, at the beginning of the nineteenth century, described it as 'a poor fishing village', and Richard Fenton saw it as 'a straggling place, meanly built, with many chasms in its strets, the mere skeleton of the town it once was.'. Camden's *Britannia* simply stated that it stood on the river Nevern and was 'call'd in British *Trevdraeth*, which signifies *the town on the sand*', and that it had been built by a Norman 'whose posterity made it a Corporation, and granted it several privileges, and constituted therein a Portrieve and a Bayliff; and also built themselves a Castle above the town.' Even George Owen, lord of Cemais, paid little regard to the town in his writings, despite the fact that it was his *caput baroniae,* and our knowledge of it in medieval times is derived from rentals and other records.

It was not until 1890 that the town received recognition when the rector, Evan Jones, published his *Historical Sketch of Newport, Pembrokeshire.* He was of 'opinion that every parish of importance should have its history written by someone,' and as he 'had the honour of being appointed Mayor' for that year and was 'unhappily precluded' from performing 'any material work of public utility,' he trusted that his monograph would 'be accepted by his fellow-burgesses and other parishioners as a small compensation for the lack of more tangible performances, as well as a pledge of his desire to animate them with a full apprehension of their obligations as inheritors of very ancient municipal privileges.' As such an inheritor, the present author had intended to offer this contribution towards extending our knowledge of the town and its people during one of his mayoral terms, but was not content to do so while so much remained unknown, nor would he now were it not that the whirligig of time demands. He hopes that it will inspire others to delve deeper into the past of this unique and historic ancient borough.

DILLWYN MILES

ACKNOWLEDGEMENT

The author wishes to acknowledge the assistance he has received in preparing this book from the Lady Marcher of Cemais, Dr. J. Geraint Jenkins, Martin Lewis, Paul Raggett, and Peter Davies, and from his brother, Herbert, and his son, Anthony. He is particularly indebted to Don Benson, Director of the Dyfed Archaeological Trust, for permission to reproduce the artist's impression of the excavated burgage plots at Newport; to Judith for her support and encouragement; to May Evans for the pleasant and efficient manner in which she typed the manuscript; to the Cultural Services Committee of the Dyfed County Council for publishing the book; to Mary John, Librarian at the County Library, Haverfordwest, who, with great thoroughness arranged for its publication, and to C. I. T., and especially Neil Davies, for taking such care in the production of the book.

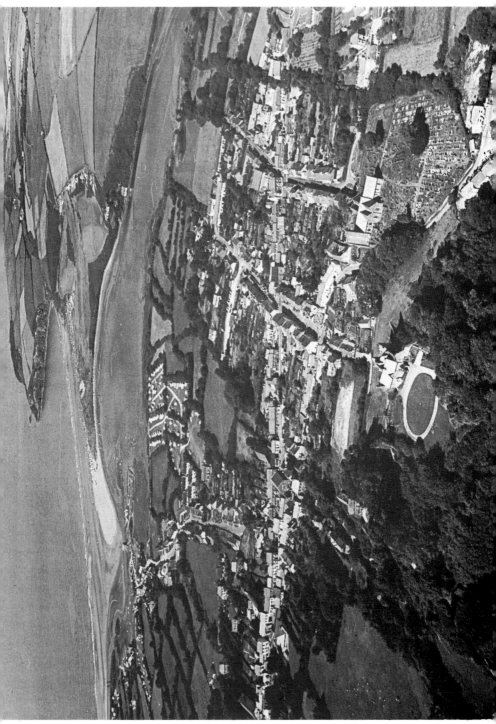

BEFORE NEWPORT

Long before the ancient borough of Newport was planted by the Normans at the foot of the castle, there was a seaside settlement on the estuary of the Nevern. It was called Trefdraeth, 'the township on the shore'. A long-held tradition that it was once 'sunk beneath the wave' can be verified, but the speculation that it stood on Traeth Mawr and was 'like another Perranzabuloe swallowed by the sands'[1] cannot be sustained.

The name first appears in 1215, in *Brut y Tywysogyon* (the Chronicle of the Princes) which records that Llywelyn the Great 'subjugated the men of Cemais and the castle of Trefdraeth ... was razed to the ground.' John Leland, on his itinerary through Wales in the 1530's stated that 'a monke of Strateflur' (Strata Florida) had told him that 'for a certenty Newport in Kemmisland is called Tredraith in Walsch,'[2] and William Camden, in his *Britannia,* made reference to 'the place call'd in British Trevdraeth, which signifies the town on the sand.'[3] In the middle of the eighteenth century, the strand is called *Traeth Edrywy,*[4] a name that finds an echo in the offshore rock *Carreg Edrywy,*[5] commonly known locally as Carreg y Drewi, 'the stinking stone'. Edrywy may have been an old name for the river, or for the district, or it may have been a tribal name.[6]

The settlement on the shore is believed to have been on the Parrog even though Lewis Morris in his plan of 'Newport Bay and Harbour', shows no trace of a habitation or other building near the estuary in 1748, and only marks *Rhyd Barrog,*[7] 'the Parrog ford'. 'Parrog' derives from the Old English *pearroc,*[8] meaning a small enclosure, or paddock, but it is applied here, as it is at Goodwick, to a low-lying area near the sea shore. The masters of vessels arriving at Swansea in 1583 were ordered 'to discharge and cast ashore upon the perroge', which indicates that the word was also used for a place where ships unloaded, as was the case at Newport up to the last war.

In the Nevern estuary sea erosion has combined with powerful tides and a strong river flow to produce a wide stretch of sand, extensive mud flats, a pebbly beach and wave-cut rock platforms, and a sand bar across the mouth of the river that has blighted the development of Newport as a port. Unrelenting on-shore winds have added their contribution by blowing sand into sand dunes that are held together by the roots of bennet, or marram, and therefore called The Bennet,[9] or else The Warren, for the Normans were believed to have kept their newly introduced rabbits there.

Apart from the Presely, and some other, hills, the county presents a landscape that largely comprises near-flat surfaces at three levels.[10] The coastal zone, at approximately two hundred feet, the so-called 200 foot platform, was cut about seventeen million years ago when the sea level was approximately two hundred feet higher than at present. Traces of a platform at 400 feet form the summit of Dinas Island, and evidence of the 600 foot surface is to be found to the north-east of Newport. When the sea was lower than it is today, the land surface reached out for seven or eight miles to the twenty fathom contour.

The cliffs on the south side of Newport Bay are Ordovician shales,

Parrog

while those on the north side are regarded as Silurian, although it is now considered that they, too, might be Ordovician.[11] The sea's constant pounding at the base of the cliffs beyond Y Cwm has left wave-cut platforms that are exposed at low tide in the bays of Traeth Samuel, Chwarel Ffeiradon, Aber Step and Traeth Brodan.

Violent volcanic activity occurred during the Ordovician period and igneous rocks are exposed in long narrow strips on the Presely Hills, among which are the spotted dolerites which contain crystals of white and pink felspar that enabled the area to be identified as the source of the 'bluestones' of Stonehenge. Carn Ingli is a great mass of igneous rocks, ranging from granodiorite to quartz-dolerite.

The great mountain building epoch, known as the Caledonian Orogeny, when ancient continents collided at the close of the Silurian period, imposed an east-north-east to west-south-west trend on the Presely Hills. Carn Ingli runs parallel with this trend, and the course of the river Nevern was determined at the same time.

On at least two occasions the area lay submerged under the Irish Sea glacier, which at one time was over three thousand feet thick.[12] The last glaciation, about 18,000 years ago, smoothed the contours by depositing a cover of glacial till, or boulder clay, that had been dredged off the floor of the Irish Sea. As the weather became less cold and the ice began to melt, meltwater flowed beneath the ice with such erosive energy that it gouged deep steep-sided channels as it rushed towards the sea. The most spectacular meltwater channel in Britain is the Gwaun Valley, which isolated Carn Ingli from the mass of the Presely Hills. Another channel all but separated Dinas Island from the mainland. The course of the Nevern was diverted when a large meltwater gorge was formed in the northern flank of the valley, leaving the pre-glacial course, from Nevern Bridge to the New Mill, abandoned.[13]

Water released from the melting ice mass caused the sea level to rise and, in so doing, it drowned the lower reaches of a river, forming a *ria*, of which Milford Haven is the classic example. The drowned lower reaches of the Nevern became Newport Bay.[14] Tree stumps that were exposed on Traeth Mawr in 1971 were shown to have been submerged in 6,350 BC, when the sea rose to its present level.

By then, man had already arrived and had settled, at least for a while, on the south bank of the Nevern, a little below the bridge. This was during the Mesolithic period, or Middle Stone Age, and the sea was probably still some miles away, so that men were able to hunt in the forest on Traeth Mawr and beyond. The little group that set up their tepee-type tents on this river bank left behind them evidence of a flint knapping site, where they had shaped flint stones, probably beach pebbles, into sharp-edged arrow heads and barbs. They left only the waste flakes that had been chipped off the core stones: 'about twenty chips and spalls of flint' were found, in July 1922, beneath the peat that rested on 'a matrix of hard grey alluvial clay', and 'about fifty pieces of flint, a few pieces of chipped felsite and numerous pieces of charcoal' were found later that year on the same site.[15]

Recent excavation by the Dyfed Archaeological Trust in the lower part of Long Street has uncovered some 170 flints, most of them waste flakes, together with a stone tranchet axe of about 7,000 BC.[16]

Cat Rock and Dinas Head.

3

A little way up the road from the bridge, hidden now behind bungalows, stands a cromlech, or burial chamber, erected by the Neolithic people who came next and settled in the vicinity about 3,500 BC.[17] It is known as *Carreg Coetan Arthur*, a name which reflects man's conjecture as to the nature and origin of such megalithic structures. Arthur, they said, had hurled its capstone there, quoit-fashion, as Samson had done at Samson's Quoit at Mathry.

Apart from a brief mention by George Owen, the Elizabethan historian and lord of Cemais, in 1603[18], the cromlech was first described by J P Wyndham in 1774.[19] He found 'the monument...quite perfect' and added that 'the upper stone is shaped like a mushroom and is upwards of nine feet in diameter.' He thought that it was 'the sepulchral monument of some great man among the Britons. The site was excavated in 1979-80.[20] On the chamber floor was a small quantity of cremated bones and charcoal, together with the remains of cremation urns. Outside the chamber was more Neolithic pottery together with a fragment of a polished axe and some flint knives and scrapers. The tomb is composed of large megaliths, most probably erratics deposited in the vicinity, with a massive capstone supported only by two of four uprights that are dug deep in the ground. The chamber was covered by a cairn revetted by a ring of boulders.

Carreg Coetan Arthur is one of a number of burial chambers to be found in, or near, the valley of the river Nevern. On the north side is the double-chambered tomb of Trellyffaint (SN 082425), the upper surface of its surviving capstone covered with cupmarks, and Llech-y-drybedd (SN 101431), which has a huge capstone supported by three uprights,

Professor Glyn Daniel at Carreg Coetan Arthur.

hence its name, 'the trivet stone'. These chambers may have heen erected by people moving to the more exposed plateau that would have been less heavily wooded. On the south side of the valley is Pentre Ifan (SN 099370), the most impressive megalithic monument in Wales and, not far away, is the unique gallery grave of Bedd-yr-afanc (SN 109346). Beyond the head of the valley, and on a route that was plainly used in prehistoric time, is Mountain Cromlech (SN 166328).

Bedd Samson, a mound beside the river above Newport Bridge, may have been named 'the grave of Samson' because it looked as though it might have been the burial place of a giant, and there is nothing else to indicate that it is other than a natural feature.

A crescent-shaped earthwork, marked 'Settlement' on the OS map (SN 058395) is known as Hen Gastell and it has been suggested that it was associated with the removal of William Martin from Nevern to Newport in 1191, but it is also held to have a prehistoric origin.

Cerrig-y-Gof (the smith's stones) (SN 037389) was described by Jacquetta Hawkes as 'an example of local idiosyncracy in megalithic structure'. It is a peculiar agglomeration of five rectangular burial chambers that has no parallel nearer than Mull Hill on the Isle of Man, or Aghnaskeagh Cairn B, in co. Louth, Ireland. Richard Fenton[21] excavated the site in about 1800. 'Having removed the lid stones of the cists, and digging down a foot through fine mould,' he wrote, 'I came to charcoal, and soon after discovered pieces of urns of the rudest pottery, some particles of bones, and a quantity of black sea pebbles. I opened them all, and with a very trifling variation of their contents found them of the same character.' He also excavated in the spaces between each chamber, as

Professor W. F. Grimes at Cerrig-y-gof.

5

well as in the centre over which, he thought, 'the Cromlech had been raised,' but found 'nothing indicatory of sepulture.' The proximity of the beach at Aber Rhigian may indicate that this was the burial site of a Neolithic community that had landed there, probably from Ireland.

To the people of this period, the Presely Hills were of special significance, if not sanctity. Polished axes of spotted dolerite were made in 'axe-factories' on the eastern end of the hills, and some were taken by axe-traders to places as far apart as Wessex and co. Antrim. It was thought at one time that the 'bluestones' that were transported from Carn Meini and Carn Alw to Salisbury Plain, eventually to become part of Stonehenge, had been taken down the shortest route, to the estuary of the Nevern, but rather than face the perils of an exposed coast and the treacherous tide-races in the sounds, they were hauled down the southern slopes to Canaston Bridge and the waters of Milford Haven.

The men who brought metal, in the form of bronze, colonised the upland areas, where they buried their dead, at first in a crouched position in cists and, later, with their cremated remains interred in cinerary urns, in each case covered with round barrows, or cairns. A cairn of this kind stands prominently on Carn Briw (SN 057371), and there are two ring cairns and a kerb cairn on Carn Edward (SN 054365).

Others are to be found on summits, such as Foel Eryr, Foel Cwm Cerwyn and Foel Drygarn, and along the trackway on the ridge of the Presely Hills, that was their trade-route to Ireland. Beakers, and then food vessels, were placed with the dead, and their burial ritual required a ring cairn, as at Glyn Gath (SN 017366), or an embanked circle, like Meini Gwyr (SN 142266), or a stone circle, such as Gors Fawr (SN 135294). Standing stones often formed part of complex ritual sites, though they were also placed as guide posts on routeways. Bedd Morus (SN 038365) stands where the road to the Gwaun Valley crosses the Presely ridgeway and, as its name suggests, it may indicate a sepulchral site. One legend states that it is the grave of Morus, a notorious robber who lurked among the surrounding rocks, while another tells of rival lovers who fought to the death for the hand of the lovely daughter of Pontfaen House and poor Morus, who lost, was buried here. It also serves as a boundary stone between the parishes of Newport and Llanychlwydog and bears the initials of a resolute lord of Cemais, Sir Thomas Davies Lloyd, Bart. (1820-77).

A settled agricultural society made territorial demands, and defensive settlements were established on hilltops and on promontories. The need for such defences was increased with the arrival of a more aggressive people, using iron tools and implements, from about 600 BC onward. They built hundreds of small, often circular, defended enclosures, over most of Pembrokeshire, as well as promontory forts, and powerful hillforts on Foel Drygarn (SN 158336), Garn Fawr (SN 896388) and on Carn Ingli.

Carn Ingli is first mentioned in the twelfth century *Life of Brynach*,[22] where it is given as *Mons Angelorum* to sustain a fiction that the saint of Nevern used to commune with the angels on the summit of the mountain, which was named after one Ingli, a giant according to George Owen, who also noted that its appearance from the east and north was 'in form like the upper part of the Greek letter Ω'[23].

Carn Ingli.

The summit, comprising two peaks separated by a saddle, is occupied by an Iron Age fortified village, with ramparts, where the scree slopes were insufficiently steep, forming a long, triangular enclosure that is divided into four sections, or extensions. The original enclosure may date from Neolithic times, but it is more likely to have been built in the Iron Age and to have been altered through long occupation. There are nine entrances to the enclosure, within which some twenty-five round or quadrangular houses were the homes of up to a hundred and fifty people. On the slopes are more hut circles, and terraced enclosures that may have been cultivation plots or paddocks. Here was a fortified village, with additional areas protected with ramparts as the population increased, that was occupied for a long period of time, and was in full use up to the middle of the first century AD. The shattered stones forming screes on the flanks of the mountain were broken off by frost action.

Carn Cŵn (SN 014383), 'the dogs' cairn', is a small outlier of Carn Ingli. Beneath a massive overhang is 'the Wishing Well' into which pins are thrown to cure warts, or to make a secret wish.

Carn Ffoi (SN 049379), 'the cairn of retreat', has a single dry-stone rampart enclosing an oval hillfort, with entrances on the south and west, and a number of hut circles along the line of the rampart.

There are no traces of coastal promontory forts nearer than Castell Treruffydd (SN 101448) and Pencastell Ceibwr (SN 111459) on the one side, and Dinas Island on the other. An inland promontory fort at Castell Henllys (SN 117390) has been excavated and reconstructed as an Iron Age site.

When the Romans arrived in Wales before the end of the first century A.D, they found a tribe called the Demetae in occupation of Demetia, as

Carn Ffoi.

Dyfed was then known. The Demetae appear to have come to terms with the invader to such an extent that the Romans kept clear of their territory, and the Roman military station of Maridunum, or Carmarthen, eventually became the *civitas* capital of their province. The Roman emperor Magnus Maximus, who came to hunt on Y Freni Fawr,[24] it was said, was charged by Gildas, the sixth century chronicler, with having allowed an Irish tribe, the Deisi, to enter Demetia and to establish a dynasty of kings that was to rule Dyfed for the next five centuries. Evidence of their occupation is found in a few place-names, such as Cnwc, from the Irish *cnocc*, 'a hill' or 'hillock', and Clydach, which not infrequently appears in Ireland in such forms as *Clodagh* denoting a turbulent stream flowing over a stony bed, and also in the ogham-inscribed stones that commemorate Vitalianus and Maglocunus son of Clutorius in Nevern church.

The earliest evidence of Christianity in Newport is found in two cross-incised stones[25] that date from the seventh or eighth century, one of which was discovered face-downward in the churchyard and now stands in a nearby garden, and the other stands in front of the west door of the church.

The Irish presence would have eased the passage of early missionaries, the so-called Celtic Saints, who, as Gildas recorded, 'sailed the Irish Sea in their coracles', and landed in creeks and bays along the north Pembrokeshire coast. It may be that the estuary of the Nevern provided a suitable landfall from which they could follow the transpeninsular route along the Nevern and Taf valleys to Carmarthen Bay.

Pilgrims on their way from St Dogmael's to St David's are believed to have used the coast road, via Moylegrove, to Newport Sands and, after fording the river Nevern at low tide, to have followed Feidr Brenin to the main Fishguard road, at the junction of which stood Capel Dewi (SN 043391). George Owen mentions Capel Dewi as one of two pilgrimage chapels in the parish of Newport. The other was Capel Curig, situated near Newport Bridge.[26]

St Curig was a saint of some importance in Ireland in the 8th-9th centuries, where he is associated with St Patrick, and his name also occurs in Scotland in that period.[27] It is possible that Newport church may have been dedicated to him before the Normans changed it to St Mary. The only other dedication to him in west Wales is Eglwys Fair a Churig (SN 202262), where the two saints are remembered. It is significant that the annual fair at Newport is known as Ffair Gurig, and that there is a well dedicated to the saint near the site of his chapel. St. Milburg's chapel stood on a site still known as Banc-y-capel (SN 072392) across the river from the New Mill.[28]

In his *Holy Wells of Wales*, Francis Jones[29] lists as wells bearing the names of saints in and around Newport, Ffynnon Gurig, Ffynnon Ddewi, near Capel Dewi, Pistyll Samson, and Ffynnon Bedr. A water-spout at the far end of Traeth Mawr is known as Pistyll Brynach (SN 053412).

Although marauding Norsemen repeatedly ravaged St David's and left Fishguard with a name derived from the Old Scandinavian *fiskigardr*, 'an enclosure for catching or keeping fish'[30], and despite the fact that, in the words of an early Welsh poet, they 'broke the bell of the monks of Llandudoch' (St Dogmael's) in 988, and reduced their monastery so that it was no more than 'the resort of wild pigs', there is no evidence that they visited Newport.

View from Carn Ffoi.

The people of north Pembrokeshire would have lived through turbulent years of internecine fratricidal warfare before the Normans came. They would have been aware, at least, of the battle fought at Pwllwdig, or Goodwick Moor, in 1078, when Trahaearn, king of Gwynedd, came to avenge the blood of Bleddyn ap Cynfyn, his cousin, whom Rhys ab Owain, prince of Deheubarth, had slain. Rhys was defeated and was driven, *The Chronicles of the Princes* tells us, 'o'er rocks and rough brakes, like a frightened stag before deer hounds'. Nor could they not have heard of the decisive skirmish at Mynydd Carn that was fought a day's march from St David's, in 1081, when Rhys ap Tewdwr and Gruffudd ap Cynan slew Trahaearn and Caradog ap Gruffudd and Meilyr ap Rhiwallon, and thereby established dynasties that were to rule in Deheubarth and Gwynedd for the next two centuries. Nor is it likely that they would have been unaware that William the Conqueror himself, that year, had made a pilgrimage to the shrine of the patron saint at St David's.

Little is known of the governance of the cantref of Cemais in the pre-Norman period, except that the leading family was that of Gwynfardd Dyfed. His son, Cuhelyn Fardd, is believed to have been in occupation of the stronghold at Nevern, and he is described in an early pedigree as a *tywysog* (prince). He is eulogised in a poem[31] of the early part of the twelfth century as 'a leader of hosts', 'a knight at the jousting-ground', a poet whose poetry 'merits a chair', 'a dispenser at the mead-banquet' and 'a master of *gwyddbwyll*', the chess-like game which the men of Cemais are reputed to be playing before the Normans came. A reference to him, in the poem, as 'a ship-fancier' and 'a treasure of a seaport' may indicate his connection with the coastal settlement of Trefdraeth.

Parrog

Cuhelyn was undoubtedly alive when Robert Fitz Martin invaded Cemais, and they would appear to have come to a working arrangement whereby Cuhelyn maintained a position of authority under the new overlord, and his descendants continued to hold influential positions within the barony. His sons, Gwrwared and Llywelyn, were granted rights of common over the Presely Hills and these rights were confirmed to their heirs in a charter granted by Nicholas Martin, lord of Cemais, some time before 1250.[32]

THE LORDS OF CEMAIS

The history of Newport is inextricably woven with that of its founders, the lords of Cemais, and no record of its past can be considered without taking account of their fortunes.

When Roger de Montgomery, Earl of Shrewsbury, swept across Wales to Pembroke in 1093, he by-passed the *cantref* of Cemais and it was left to another Norman, whose family had already settled in Devon, to undertake its conquest. The earliest recorded reference to its invasion is that of John Leland, the King's Antiquary, who visited Wales between 1536 and 1539 and, in his report stated: 'the chaunter of S. Davides tolde me that one Martinus de Turribus, a Norman, wan the countrey of Kemmeys in Wales about the tyme of King William Conqueror.' There is no historical account of Martinus de Turribus, or Martin de Tours, as he is otherwise known probably due to confusion with the name of the saint of that appellation. There was, however, a man called Martin who was the husband of Geva, daughter and co-heir of Serlo de Burci, a prominent landholder in the West Country, but he was dead by 1086, when Geva was married to William de Falaise,[1] who held lands in Somerset, Devon and Dorset.

Cemais was occupied by Robert, the son of Martin and Geva, who is presumed to have landed in the Nevern estuary[2] some time after 1093 and before 1108. In that year Gerald de Windsor, the royal custodian of Pembroke, occupied the *cantref* of Emlyn, to the east, and the Flemings settled in the *cantrefi* of Daugleddau and Rhos to the south of Cemais.[3]

Robert is an established figure to whom there is reference in a Papal Bull of 1128 and in a Pipe Roll of 1130, and he was also known as a supporter of the Empress Matilda in 1141.[4] He built a castle at Nevern, on a site that may have been that of a promontory fort. The original castle was probably a ringwork,[5] and it was further fortified, in all likelihood by the Welsh, by the construction of a motte and outer bank and an inner stone castle ward isolated by a cut ditch.[6]

By 1115 Robert FitzMartin had given the church at Llandudoch[7] to the abbey of Tiron, in the diocese of Chartres, and had brought monks from that abbey to establish the priory of St. Dogmael's. In 1120 he obtained the consent of the abbot of Tiron for the priory to be raised to the status of an abbey, which he and his mother, Geva, endowed with lands in Wales, Devon and Ireland, and with the island of Caldey.[8]

Robert married Matilda, daughter of William Peverel of Tregamon, near Bodmin, but she is believed to have died without issue and he is said to have then married Adalesia, or Alice, daughter of Roger de Nonant of Broad Clyst, by whom he had a son, William, who succeeded him at his death in about 1159.[9]

When Henry I died, in 1135, revolt broke out in various parts of Wales. In the following year, a strong Anglo-Norman and Flemish force was severely defeated at Crug Mawr, north of Cardigan, and that town was destroyed, apart from its castle. It was not until the accession of Henry II, in 1154, that Rhys ap Gruffydd, prince of Deheubarth, had to make submission to the king,[10] and the Anglo-Normans were restored. The Welsh rose again in 1163 and, two years later, Henry launched an expedition into Wales which failed to achieve its objective. Rhys was able to recapture Cardigan and Cilgerran, but he had to do homage when Henry came to Pembroke on his way to Ireland in 1171, and the king, in return, appointed him justiciar, on his behalf, 'in all Deheubarth'. Rhys made Cardigan his chief residence,[11] and there he held the first recorded *eisteddfod*, in 1176. It was there, also, that he received Archbishop Baldwin of Canterbury and Giraldus Cambrensis on their tour of Wales, preaching the Third Crusade, in 1188.

Rhys, conscious of the strategic position of the lordship of Cemais on his southern flank,[12] concluded a solemn peace with its lord, William, son of Robert FitzMartin, and, furthermore, gave him the hand of his daughter, Angharad, in marriage.[13] Giraldus Cambrensis was justifiably outraged[14] when Rhys, his near kinsman though he was, besieged Nevern Castle and took it from his son-in-law in 1191 'in direct contravention of a whole series of oaths which he had sworn in person on the most precious relics to the effect that William should be left in all peace and security in his castle.'

Rhys gave Nevern to his eldest son, and heir, Gruffydd but, by 1194, it was in the hands of Gruffydd's hostile brother, Maelgwn, who, together with his other brother Hywel Sais, imprisoned their father within the castle,[15] which Giraldus regarded as just retribution for his conduct towards his son-in-law. Rhys was not long held,[16] however, for he was released by Hywel who, fearing a resurgence among the Anglo-Normans, destroyed Nevern Castle lest it should fall into their hands,[17] in 1195.

Rhys died in 1197 and, in 1199, Maelgwn surrendered Cardigan Castle to the king. In 1204, Hywel Sais was killed in an ambush by Maelgwn's men and, in the same year, William Marshal, Earl of Pembroke, seized Cilgerran, which undoubtedly helped William Martin to re-establish himself in Cemais and enabled him to build, or re-fortify the castle at Newport.

William Martin died in 1209 and was succeeded by his son, William, of whom little is known although he appears to be the one who gave the town of Newport its charter. He married Avice, sister of Fawkes de Breauté, a Norman adventurer who had occupied north Ceredigion and had built a castle at Aberystwyth, and by her, William had a son, Nicholas Martin. Nicholas was an infant when his father died in 1216 and he became a ward of his uncle, Fawkes, but when Fawkes fell out of royal favour in 1224, Nicholas became the ward of Henry de Trubleville, a former seneschal of Gascony.[18]

Nicholas remained in wardship until 1231, at least. In about 1240 he confirmed the charter granted to the town by his father and, by 1265, he was custodian of Cilgerran Castle. He refused to acknowledge the overlordship of the earldom of Pembroke to which the lords of Cemais were subject since the lordship had been recovered following the seizure of Cardigan and Cilgerran by William Marshal the Younger, Earl of pembroke, in 1223, or even since the capture of Cilgerran by the elder William Marshal in 1204. Nicholas was made to do 'suit and service which he owed by tenure of his lordship' of Cemais and, in 1277, he concluded an agreement with William de Valence, Earl of Pembroke, whereby the lords of Cemais were given cognizance of certain pleas, but the earl reserved for himself all pleas of the Crown and the issue of writs in Cemais.[19]

Nicholas Martin, by his first wife, whose name is not known, had two sons, Nicholas, his heir, and Robert.[20] By his second wife, Isabel, widow of Hugh Peverel, he had Warin, who became deputy justiciar of south Wales, and David, who was appointed bishop of St. David's in 1323.[21]

When Nicholas died, in 1282, he was succeeded by his son Nicholas who married Maud, daughter and heiress of Sir Guy de Brian, lord of Laugharne, and Eve, daughter of Henry de Traci, lord of Barnstaple, by whom he had a son, William. Nicholas the younger died during the lifetime of his father who was then succeeded by his grandson, William, who also inherited the lordship of Barnstaple from his mother.

William Martin married Eleanor FitzPiers, who was the widow of Sir John de Mohun of Dunster.[22] He, again, endeavoured to withdraw suit and service from the earldom of Pembroke and, although a composition was made, in 1290, between him and William de Valence, similar to the agreement of 1277, he persisted in his efforts and took his claim before the king, Edward I, at his hunting lodge at Clipston, in the Sherwood Forest, but unsuccessfully.[23] He was summoned to Parliament in 1295 by tenure of his barony of Cemais.[24] His name and seal were appended to the Barons' letter to the Pope in 1301, and in 1310 he was one of the Lords Ordainers appointed to reform the realm.[25] In the following year the king had to commission him and Hugh Courtenay to search for Piers Gaveston who was 'supposed to be hiding and wandering from place to place' in the west of England.[26] He was made justiciar of south Wales in 1315.[27] He died in 1324 and was succeeded by his son William, who was summoned to Parliament that year. William married Margaret, daughter of John, Lord Hastings, but he died leaving no issue, in 1326, having drowned, it is said, in the moat of Barnstaple Castle as he returned from a stag hunt, late at night, after the drawbridge had been raised.[28] The people of Combe Martin state that it happened in their town and that a knight on a white horse is sometimes seen there, in the light of the moon.

The barony fell into abeyance between William Martin's sisters and co-heirs, Eleanor, wife of Philip de Columbers of Nether Stowey, and Joan, wife of Nicholas, Lord Audley of Heleigh in Staffordshire.[29] As Eleanor had no children, the lordship of Cemais passed to James Audley, the son and heir of Nicholas and Joan Audley, who was only three years of age at the time. Cemais, and other Martin lands, were held in dower by Margaret, William Martin's widow, until her death in 1359. James settled the lordship of Cemais on his son Nicholas in 1374,[30] although the latter appears to have been in possession of Newport Castle by 1370, when he was ordered to fortify both Newport and Llandovery, which he had inherited through the Audleys, against invasion by the French. In 1376, the king, who held Pembroke during the nonage of John Hastings, commanded him, and his wife, Elizabeth, daughter of Henry, Lord Beaumont, 'under pain of forfeiture to do their suit to the county of Pembroke' as they were bound to do in accordance with the agreements made in 1277 and 1290.[31] In 1380 he was appointed to supervise the royal castles in Wales and, two years later, he became justiciar of south Wales.[32] He died in 1391, leaving no issue. His wife, Elizabeth, held the

14

lordship of Cemais until her death in 1401 when it passed to John Touchet, Lord Audley, the son of Nicholas's sister, Joan, and her husband, Sir John Touchet. The *inquisitio post mortem* of John Touchet, held after his death in 1409, stated that 'the revenue of the Castle and Lordship of Newport in Cammoys, £33, was a half and no more, because it had been destroyed by the invasion of the King's rebels.'

John Touchet and his wife, Isabel, had a son, James Touchet, Lord Audley and lord of Cemais and of Llandovery. He married Margaret, daughter of William de Ros of Hamlake. He was appointed justiciar of south Wales in 1423, and acted as steward of Pembroke in 1426, when Humphrey, Duke of Gloucester was earl, and he presided over the Great Sessions in 1424 and in 1436.[33] He supported the Lancastrians during the Wars of the Roses and raised 10,000 men for Henry VI, but he was ambushed, and killed, at the battle of Blore Heath on 23 September 1459.

He was succeeded by his son, John Touchet, Lord Audley, who married Anne, daughter of Sir Thomas Itchingham, by whom he had a son, James, who succeeded him at his death in 1491. James married Joan, daughter of Sir Fulke Bourchier, Lord Fitzwarine. In 1497, when the king wanted to raise more money in order to pursue the wars against the Scots, a band of Cornishmen marched to London to petition the king.[34] Audley joined them at Wells and, after a brief encounter with the king's men near Guildford, they set up camp at Blackheath where the royal army descended upon them. Audley was captured and, having been found guilty of treason, he was drawn, 'with a cote armour upon him of papir, all torne' from Newgate to Tower Hill where he was beheaded, and his head was displayed on London Bridge. His lands and titles became forfeit to the Crown, and the barony of Cemais was leased to Sir Walter Herbert, who appointed William ab Owen, possibly of Pentre Ifan, as clerk of the lordship and its courts.[35]

Lord Audley's son, John Touchet, was restored the barony of Heleigh and the lordship of Cemais in 1513. He appointed his 'trustie and well-belovyd frend', Sir James ab Owen of Pentre Ifan, steward of Cemais,[36] and he made William Owen of Henllys,whom he had met in London, clerk of the courts.[37] He had been considerably impoverished by the forfeiture of his father's estates and he was able to borrow money from William Owen as he became increasingly financially distressed. In November 1523 he made Owen 'a bargain and sale of the barony of Cemais with condition of redemption upon payment of £300' but the conveyance of the barony did not take place until 1542, [38] when Audley bid the tenantry to render all homage and fealty and to pay all customs and dues to the new lord of Cemais, William Owen.

The collection of dues had been rather neglected under the Audleys, whose interests lay mainly elsewhere, and by 1532 the rents of the barony were rendered as 'nil', and the castle was reported to be in a ruinous state. Even so, it served to keep the baronial records until they were removed by William Owen's brother, John ap Rhys ab Owen, who had been appointed recorder of the barony. He stored them at his daughter's house at Newport but, in 1558, the house was set on fire, in an attempt, it was thought, to destroy William Owen's title to the lordship.

William Owen was born in about 1488, the son of Rhys ab Owen of Henllys, whose family had held land in that vicinity since the thirteenth century.[39] Rhys ab Owen had married Jane, daughter of Phillip Elliot of Earwear, at St. Lawrence parish church on 20 July 1487. She was the widow of Philip ap Gwilym of Stone Hall, who had died the previous year leaving her with four young children, and it is likely that William was born there. He was admitted to the Middle Temple in 1514 and, in 1521, he published an abridgement of the statutes of England, which was the first book written by a Welshman to be published in this country.[40]

Owen had settled at Pembroke by 1522 and he was mayor of the borough five years later.[41] He held various offices in the county and practised as lawyer in Bristol at the same time. He married Margaret Henton, a widow of London and when she died, without issue, he took, as his second wife, Elizabeth, daughter of Sir George Herbert of Swansea, by whom he had a son, George, and a daughter, Katherine, who married Owen Johns of Trecwn.[42] He also had nine illegitimate children, five of whom were by his mistress Jane Lee of Salop. He died in 1574, having already made a settlement granting to his son, George, the 'castle and lordship of Newport in Kemes with its appurtenances'.

George Owen was born at Henllys, probably in 1552, but nothing is known of his early life and there is no record of his education before he was admitted to Barnard's Inn in 1573. By then he had been married for two years to Elizabeth, daughter of William Philipps of Picton Castle by his wife Janet, sister of Sir John Perrot. Elizabeth gave birth to ten children and, after her death in 1606, Owen married Ancred, or Angharad, daughter of William Obiled of Carmarthen, his mistress of long standing who had borne him seven illegitimate children. After their marriage she gave birth to another six children, among whom were George Owen, York Herald, and Evan Owen, rector of Newport and, later, chancellor of St. David's.

George Owen was one of the greatest Welshmen of his day.[43] His main interest lay in the land, and in his lordship of Cemais. As an agriculturist he advocated good husbandry and introduced new methods of improving the land. He urged a revival of the use of marl and, insodoing, gave the earliest known description of glacial till, or boulder clay, and furthered the practice of liming the land by tracing the limestone veins and coal seams, thus becoming an innovator in the study of geology. He prepared a map of Pembrokeshire, which William Camden used in his *Britannia,* and he produced a pamphlet outlining the defences of Milford Haven for the Queen. His ambition to prove that the lordship of Cemais had come to his father by descent, rather than by purchase, made of him a 'creative' genealogist, and he was not above inventing a coat of arms for himself. His endeavours to restore out-dated customs and dues enraged his tenancy, and made the burgesses of Newport obdurate, and caused him to spend a considerable part of his life in litigation. He diligently exercised his public duties, as a magistrate, a deputy lieutenant and as a deputy vice-admiral of south Wales. He was sheriff in 1587 and in 1602. His permanent contribution was a corpus of written work, chief among which was his *Description of Penbrokshire* that gave a comprehensive portrait of the county in the Elizabethan age.

He died on 26 August 1613, at Haverfordwest, at the house of his daughter, Elizabeth, whose husband was mayor of the town that year. He was buried in Nevern church where he is commemorated on a brass plate.

He was succeeded by his only surviving legitimate son, Alban Owen of Henllys.[44] Alban married, successively, Lettice Mercer, step-daughter of Thomas Revell of Forest, Cilgerran; Elizabeth Owen of Dolgellau, and Joan daughter of William Bradshaw of St Dogmael"s.[45] He was settled, when he first married, by his father at Berry Hill and at Court, Eglwyswrw, where a new house was built on the site of the old moated manor house. He pursued his father's efforts to exercise feudal rights, and he was active as a justice of the peace, a deputy lieutenant and as sheriff in 1608, and again in 1643. Two sons by his first wife died young and there was only to succeed him his son, David, by his third wife.

David Owen married Anne, daughter of Robert Corbet of Ynysymaengwyn in Merioneth in about 1651 and, by her, he had a son, William, but as he died without issue, the lordship was conveyed to his daughters, Elizabeth, who married Arthur Laugharne of Llanrheithan, and Anne, wife of Thomas Lloyd of Penpedwast, and their heirs. Anne and her husband had a son, William Lloyd of Penpedwast, who married Jane, daughter of Owen Ford of Berry Hill and, by her, had three daughters, the eldest of whom, Anne Lloyd, became the wife of Thomas Lloyd of Bronwydd. In 1751 Thomas and Anne Lloyd purchased the moiety of the barony of Cemais held by John Laugharne of Llanrheithan for £2,000.

Anne Lloyd was succeeded by her son, Thomas Lloyd of Bronwydd (1740-1807) who served as a captain in the 10th Foot Regiment and, later, as colonel of the Fishguard and Newport Regiment. He married Mary, daughter of Dr John Jones of Haverfordwest and was succeeded at his death by his son, Thomas Lloyd (1788-1845), who married Anne Davies Thomas, daughter of John Thomas of Llwydcoed and Llety-mawr in the county of Carmarthen. He was succeeded by the eldest of his five sons, Thomas Davies Lloyd.

Thomas Davies Lloyd was born in 1820 and was educated at Harrow and Christ College, Oxford.[46] He joined the 13th Light Dragoons and was serving with the 82nd Foot Regiment in Canada when he received news of his father's death, in 1845. He returned to this country and, a year later, was married to Henrietta Mary, daughter of George Reid of Bunkers Hill, Jamaica, and Watlington Hall, Norfolk, by his wife Louisa Inge of Plas Tanybwlch. He took great interest in the affairs of the barony and unsuccessfully claimed the Martin peerage and a seat in the House of Lords. He arranged a perambulation of the boundaries of Cemais and had his initials, T D LL, carved on boundary stones. He was Liberal Member of Parliament for Cardiganshire from 1865 to 1874 and was sheriff of that county in 1851, and a deputy lieutenant. He received a baronetcy in 1863. He rebuilt Bronwydd in 1853 'as a romantic Rhineland castle',[47] and had the same architect, R K Penson, to convert the gatehouse of Newport Castle into a residence, in 1859. He died in 1876, leaving mortgage debts of £94,000 which faced his only son, Marteine Owen Mowbray Lloyd who succeeded him.

17

Marteine Lloyd was educated at Eton and was commissioned in the Pembroke Yeomanry Cavalry. He married Katharine Helena, daughter of Alexander Dennistoun of Golf Hill, co. Lanark, in 1878. He was sheriff of Cardiganshire in 1881 and was a magistrate and a deputy lieutenant. Sir Marteine's only son, Martin Kemes Arundel, was killed on the Somme in 1916 and the succession passed to his sister, Nesta Constance Muriel, on Sir Marteine's death in 1933. Nesta was married to Frederick Edward Withington of Bicester and was succeeded, when she died in 1943, by her daughter, Morfa Audley. At her death, without issue in 1958, the succession passed to her aunt, Joan Henllys, wife of Major General Philip Saxon Gregson-Ellis, who died in 1973 and was succeeded by her daughter, Hyacinthe Nairne Marteine, wife of John Hawkesworth.

NEWPORT CASTLE

Newport Castle was built by William Martin after he had been driven out of Nevern by his father-in-law, Rhys ap Gruffydd, The Lord Rhys, in 1191[1]. Rhys had secured his castle of Cardigan from the south by giving his daughter, Angharad, in marriage to William Martin, as he had protected his eastern flank by marrying his son and heir, Gruffydd, to a daughter of William de Braose, lord of Radnor and Builth. And although he had acknowledged the sovereignty of Henry II and had been rewarded by being made Justiciar of South Wales, when the king died in 1189 he felt released from his bond and set out to wage war on the Anglo-Normans. He began a series of lightning raids on their lordships and the taking of Nevern was a part of this campaign.

After the death of The Lord Rhys in April 1197, the succession of Gruffydd was recognised by Archbishop Hubert of Canterbury, the Justiciar, on behalf of the king.[2] Maelgwn took him prisoner shortly afterwards but he was free again the following year when he recovered Ceredigion, except for Cardigan, and in 1199 he captured Cilgerran. Maelgwn now turned to the king who, on 3 December that year, conferred upon him by charter both Ceredigion and the cantref of Emlyn on condition that he surrendered to the Crown the castle of Cardigan and the adjoining land on the north side of the Teifi estuary. Hywel Sais, who was so called because he had been held hostage at the court of Henry II, was treacherously killed, in his cantref of Cemais, by Maelgwn's men in 1204. In the same year William Marshal captured Cilgerran, and Cemais was restored to William Martin.

In 1197-98 William Martin obtained a loan of twenty marks from the Crown, by the hand of Archbishop Hubert, on account of King Richard's absence in France, towards 'rebuilding the castle of Cammeis'.[3] It has been maintained that this money was used to rebuild Nevern Castle, but the evidence shows that Cemais remained in the possession of The Lord Rhys's sons until 1204.[4] If it refers to Newport Castle, on the other hand, it suggests that Martin had established his castle at Newport not long after his eviction from Nevern.[5]

Newport Castle: Buck 1740.

Sir Richard Colt Hoare c 1810.

William Martin built his castle[6] on a natural spur overlooking the estuary of the Nevern. It was of the ringwork type, rather than a motte, cut off on the south side by a wide, deep ditch that formed a moat which probably extended all round the castle at one time.[7]

Gastineau 1824

Newport Castle is first mentioned in 1215 when it was taken and razed to the ground by Llywelyn ap Iorwerth.[8] It was recovered in April 1223 when William Marshal the Younger, Earl of Pembroke, landed at Porthclais with an army that he had mustered in Ireland, and recaptured Cardigan and Cilgerran.

In 1257 Llywelyn ap Gruffudd, joined by the descendants of The Lord Rhys, swept over south-west Wales, but Newport was the only castle they were able to take.[9] There is no evidence that they could retain a hold on Cemais.[10]

The castle destroyed by Llywelyn was probably still made of tirnber and the present remains are those of the castle that was built after the raid. That there was a substantial building in existence by 1277 is indicated in a staternent by George Owen that 'it appeareth by an auncient and faire composicion made betweene the Lorde of Kemes and his ten[an]tes....that the lord had a gaole for felons in his castle at Newporte, and that all felons taken in Kemes were brought thether.'[11]

The towers and a small portion of the curtain wall date from the end of the thirteenth century, or the beginning of the next. The rest belong to the nineteenth century.[12]

In 1370 Nicholas Audley, lord of Cemais, was ordered by the king to fortify the castle in view of the threat of a French invasion.[13] In 1395 the sum of 66s.1d. (£3.30) was spent on carting lime from Haverfordwest to make mortar, and for stone tiles and lath-nails and the wages of a mason, a tiler and workers to carry out repairs to the castle.[14] Three years later, a stone mason was paid 4d. a day for sixteen days, and his assistant 3d. a day, for repairing the castle, and two carpenters received 5d. a day for felling timber for three days in Pencelli Forest for the purpose of making

Fielding after Price Carter Edwards 1832.

21

a new bridge for the castle, and planks were brought from Fishguard at a cost of 6s., with 8d. for their carriage.[15] The castle was, at that time, in the care of the constable of Cemais, Llewelyn ab Owen, who received 40s. per annum for his services.

In 1409 the castle was 'valued at a half its worth, £33', on account of damage suffered during the revolt of Owain Glyndŵr.

The rental of 1583[16] states that the castle was 'presentlie in utter ruyne and decay and hath been so for a long tyme and is not valued at anything in the rent rowles.' Despite its ruinous condition, it would appear that some part could be put to some use as it is known that the records of the barony were kept there until the steward,[17] John ab Owen, the brother of William Owen, lord of Cemais, removed them to the house of his daughter in Newport in 1556, which was then burned down, probably deliberately in an attempt to destroy the lord's possessory title. Then, in 1588, an exemplification of the records was signed by the steward, Owen Johns of Trecwn, on 20 October that year at Newport Castle,[18] and even as late as 1639 the *inquisito post mortem* of John Lloyd of Hendre and Cwmgloyn was held 'at the castle'.[19]

The castle remained in a ruined state until 1859 when the gatehouse was converted into a residence, and its curtain wall repaired. It comprises four works upon the curtain: on the north-west the Hunters' Tower, on the south-west the Kitchen Tower, on the south-east the Great Tower, and on the north-east the Gatehouse.

The Hunters' Tower was described, following the visit of the Cambrian Archaeological Association in 1859,[20] as 'the great banqueting hall of the castle', but the 1594 extent stated that it was used 'for keepinge of the lordes howndes' and 'was called Hunters Towre'.[21] Only the western flank of the tower stands to its full height.[22] There are traces of a mantel and fireplace on the first floor, and there is the circular shaft of a well at the north end of the wall. At the angle with the curtain, in the thickness of the wall, are two small chambers, one containing a latrine that was used as a privy until fairly recent times. A short piece of the curtain extending south from the tower is medieval.

The Kitchen Tower, so-called because the Royal Commission on Ancient Monuments thought, in 1925,[23] that it had seen an oven there, has virtually disappeared. A semi-subterranean chamber of a later date, discovered in 1867 and containing human remains and a knife blade, was renovated in 1871.[24] The soffit of the lintel slab is inscribed: *Gosodwyd y garreg hon gan James Salmon, Awst 19eg. 1871. Bu farw Awst 21ain. 1871,* commemorating the fact that the stone had been laid by James Salmon on 19 August 1871, and that he had died two days later.[25] The internal walls of the chamber are built of slabs set in a herring-bone pattern and there is a light-shaft, with an iron grill, in the roof vault, which may have led to the belief that here was 'the gaole as well for felons and other persons' mentioned by George Owen.[26]

The Great Tower has a large D-shaped chamber the entrance to which from the inner ward is through a short passage.[27] An external stair-turret led to the upper storeys. The interior has an alcove on the east side and blocked light-bays on the south and west. The large niches in the north wall were probably cupboards, and there is a small niche near the door.

Hanslip Fletcher 1948.

In the south-east corner a blocked passage to an external light may have contained a garderobe. Near its entrance is a refuse-shute, and there is another in the east alcove, both dischaging into a latrine-tank below. The first floor also has alcoves and niches, and there are traces of a second floor.

Adjoining the tower is another building at the base of which is an undercroft having a rib-vaulted chamber with a central pillar, carved in the thirteenth century, from which spring eight arches that terminate in as many pilasters. When the chamber was being cleared out, in 1858, a jug and a two-handled bowl, probably made in the pottery kiln now beneath the Memorial Hall, were discovered. The chamber has been held to have been the undercroft of a chapel, and is therefore known as 'The Crypt', but an inspection of the chamber above it provides no evidence of such a use.

The Gatehouse had two D-shaped towers flanking a covered entrance. The eastern tower is shown to be in a ruinous condition in the 1740 print by Nathaniel and Samuel Buck, and it was reduced to its lowest storey when the gatehouse was converted into a residence in 1859. The western tower rises in three storeys above the base, the lower two of which are D-shaped and the third is polygonal, and a corbel table above it supports a hexagonal wall that was formerly crenellated.

The conversion of the gatehouse into a residence was carried out in 1859 by James Salmon to a design by R Kyrke Penson, the architect employed by Sir Thomas Davies Lloyd to rebuild his mansion, Bronwydd, in the parish of Llangynllo in Carmarthenshire six years previously. The residence was extended on its east side in about 1890 under the direction of David Jekins, the Llandeilo architect, and the curtain raised on either side of the house.[28]

Newport Castle from St Mary's churchyard.

THE BOROUGH

Newport came into being as a planted borough created by William Martin, lord of Cemais, in the shadow of the castle he had built following his eviction from Nevern in 1191.[1] In view of the precarious hold of the Martins over Cemais, it is difficult to know when the town was incorporated. It has been suggested by some modern historians that it obtained its first charter in 1197, in which case it would have been granted by its founder, but the earliest record of a charter is of that granted by his son, William Martin II, which he must have sealed some time before 1215 when Llewelyn the Great captured Cemais and destroyed Newport Castle. The charter of his son, Nicholas Martin, which may be attributed to about 1241, was, as he made clear, a confirmation of the privileges granted to the burgesses by his father:

KNOW ye, present and to come, that I, Nicholas, son of William Martin, lord of Cemais, have given and granted, and by this my charter, have confirmed to my burgesses of Newport, all the liberties and customs written hereunder, which William FitzMartin, my father, to the same did grant and give by his charter, that is to say, that they shall have common of pasture in my land and common in water from the ditch which encloses the town towards the east as far as the sea, and easement of wood for their houses and buildings and for their fires under the supervision of the forester. Likewise, if a burgess die from any death whatsoever, unless he lose his life by judgement for felony, I shall have nothing of his chattels, except the relief, which is 12d. Likewise, if a burgess deliver to any man his living plough cattle and the latter lose his life, being accused of felony or larceny, the burgess shall prove the cattle to be his, by good and lawful men, and shall have them. Likewise, if a burgess hath hired land of any freeman, and the freeman wish to break the agreement, I ought to distrain therefore for the holding of the agreement. In the same manner I ought to distrain the debtors of the burgesses, of whom they have bail and witnesses, and make them pay their debts. Likewise, a burgess accused by any foreigner shall be bailed by his neighbours. Likewise, they ought to have a reeve and a catchpole, appointed by consultation between me and them. Likewise, no foreign merchant may buy or sell out of my borough of Newport. Likewise, a burgess accused of felony or larceny and says 'I deny the felony or larceny and whatever is charged against me' makes a good defence. Likewise, the burgesses shall not go on expedition except as the burgesses of Pembroke go. Likewise, with the aforesaid liberties, I have granted them all the liberties and good customs of Pembroke, all which said liberties I have granted and confirmed to them and to their heirs, to be held and had of me, and of my heirs, freely and entirely and peaceably, and that this my gift and grant and confirmation may be firm and steadfast for ever, to this charter I have put my seal, these being witnesses: Lord John de Arundel, John de Cantington, Robert ab Owen, William ap Gwrwared, then constable, David ab Owen, Henry Goeg, William...., Howel ab Evan Meredith, clerk, and many others.[2]

Nicholas was an infant when his father died in 1216, in ward to his uncle, Fawkes de Breauté, who held Glamorgan for the Crown and, having occupied north Ceredigion, built Aberystwyth Castle.

When William Marshal the Younger, Earl of Pembroke, recaptured Cardigan in 1223, it is assumed that he also drove the Welsh out of Cemais. The lordship was, at the time, in the hands of the Crown, due to Nicholas's nonage and, in 1226, it was placed in the charge of William Marshal by the king, Henry III, while he conducted an enquiry to determine whether it was held of the Crown or of the earldom of Pembroke.[3] Nicholas was still a ward in 1231 but he was in possession of Cemais by 1241, when he set his seal to the confirmation of his father's charter.[4]

In 1257 Newport Castle was destroyed by Llewelyn the Last.[5] Nicholas was taken prisoner and his tenants were exhorted by the king to contribute to his ransom.[6] He was constable of Cilgerran Castle by 1265 and was accused, in 1275,[7] of having taken timber from Cilgerran forest for the purpose of building a mill at Newport. The mill was built near the castle for protection against enemy attack.

At some unspecified date he exchanged Newport Castle for the manor of Kingston, in Devon, with Sir John Peverel for the term of the latter's life.[8] Sir John was his step-son, being the son of Hugh Peverel of

Town Charter c1241.

26

Ermington whose relict, Isabel, had become Nicholas's second wife. In 1280 Peverel presented the living of Ermington, near Kingston, to his half-brother David Martin, who later became bishop of St David's.

In about 1278 Nicholas granted a further charter to the burgesses of Newport in which he specified the boundaries of the liberties and defined their rights of pasture and tenure:

KNOW ye, present and to come, that I, Nicholas son of William Martin, lord of Cemais, have given and granted and by this my charter have confirmed to my burgesses of Newport in Cemais in common all my land wet and dry, moors and turbaries, without their burgages and within, according to these boundaries, namely, on the east part of the town of Newport from the chapel of [Saint] Milburg as the Clydach holds its course as far as the boundaries of the lands of the sons of William Dev towards Dolrannog, saving to me and my heirs the dry arable land in the place called Gwern-y-rhaw and also saving whatever arable land there may be between Gwern-y-rhaw and Carn Ingli within the bounds of Dolrannog. And saving to the burgesses and their heirs and assigns all the pasture in the same land so long as it is not ploughed or bearing corn. And I grant on behalf of myself and my heirs and assigns that that land shall not be sold to any foreigner but only to my burgesses of Newport. And from the boundaries of the lands of the sons of William Dev as far as the boundaries of the lands of Dolrannog and thus encircling the mountain called Carn Ingli as far as the boundaries of the tenement of Nantmarchan. And thence as far as the boundaries of Mynyddmelin. And thence descending the highway leading from Newport to Haverford to the river west of Park-y-marriage running towards Rhigian as far as the sea, saving the burgages and the lands of freeholders and the lands of burgesses within the aforesaid boundaries and saving the lands of those bearing a free rent outside their burgages. And thence all the marshland on both sides of the river called Nevern as far as the bridge of the town of Newport over the Nevern and the small island which is between the said bridge and the lord's mill called New Mill. Moreover, I grant to my burgesses, their heirs and assigns, that they may collect fern through all my demesne, namely, at Bury, at Rhigian and Park-y-marriage, outside my corn in the time of summer and autumn.[9]

The charter was witnessed by Llewelyn Goch, constable of Cemais; Richard Suetman, prepositus of Newport; Eynon ap Gwilym ap Gwrwared, David Foel ap David ab Owen, . . . ap Llewelyn ab Owen, John Cole, Iorwerth Foel ap Gwrnerth, 'and many others'. This was the first reference to the *prepositus* or *portreeve*, or mayor, of Newport by name.

At the inquisition on the death of Nicholas Martin in 1282 it was returned that Newport was held of William Marshal, Earl of Pembroke and Earl Marshal.[10] After the death of Anselm, the last of William Marshal's five sons to die without issue, Newport, and the lordship of Cemais, passed to his sister Maud, wife of Hugh Bigod, Earl of Norfolk. She also inherited the manor of Hampstead Marshall in Berkshire, and the office of Earl Marshal, which thus passed to the Earls, and later Dukes, of Norfolk.

On 8 July 1284 John Pecham, Archbishop of Canterbury, who once said that the rest of the world scarcely knew that the Welsh were a people, and who now was making his first visit to the Principality, called at Newport long enough to write a letter to the king, Edward I. In this letter he expressed his concern about the morals of the Welsh and urged that they be encouraged to settle in towns, as the Burgundians had been driven to do by the Romans, and to send their children to England to be educated.[11]

James, Lord Audley, granted a lease of the Castle Mill, the mill near Newport Bridge and New Mill in 1338 at a rental of £10 per annum, to Phillip de Hankeston, whom he later appointed constable of Cemais.[12] Audley's commitment in other direction is likely to have accounted for his action in farming the issues of the town, in 1341, to Philip de Chetwinde for the term of his life at seventeen and a half marks annually.[13] The town was farmed again in 1497, at the attainder of James Touchet, Lord Audley, to Sir Walter Herbert.

Newport ranked among the larger of the medieval towns of Wales,[14] with burgages along streets[15] that extended from the castle to the estuary of the river Nevern, and down to the bridge at Penybont, and along Goat Street and West Street on both sides of the street, and the layout of the town has remained unchanged since its inception. Two main streets run north from the castle and the church: *Longus Vicus* (Long Street) reached from the foot of the castle and *Vicus beate Marie virg'* (St Mary Street) from the church, down to the estuary at The Marsh. *Vicus caprarum* (Goat Street) remains the same, except that it ran a little further eastward. *Vicus pontis* referred not to the present Bridge Street but to the Pen-y-bont road, and at the top of that road was *Vicus Mabudrud* (Mabudrud Street).

These names appear in the extent of the town of Newport 'together with a terrier or rental of the same', made 'by the oath of William Voill' and other jurors, with 'John Picton, reeve there, and Thomas Devonald, clerk there, by the precept of Ievan ap Llewelyn ap Oweyn, seneschal of James Daudli, lord of Kemmeis on the feast of St Hilary [13 January] 12 Henry VI' [1434].

East Street is marked on an estate map of 1758 as Rocke Street, which may be a misrendering of Crog Street, where *crog* means 'a cross'. There are references to Cross Street, and also to Cross Lane and Crog Lane, implying a street near, or leading to, The Cross. Crog Lane may have been further corrupted as Cock Lane, the site of which has long been a mystery. Its central situation is indicated by the frequency with which it was quoted in the courts as the location of business transactions and of some scandalous utterings.

The upper part of Long Street has appeared in the records as High Street and as North Street, as well as by its present name, Market Street. Its topmost part became Castle Street.

Among the reasons adduced by George Owen to prove 'that Normans and Englishmen in olde tyme inhabited Newport towne', was the presence of so many English surnames,[16] and he quotes such names as Mendus, Devonald, Revell, Dyer, Runwey, Gentle, Cotton, Picton, Lopin, Chaplain, Aylman, Tucker, Belward, Jordan, Herring 'and manye such which plainelye sheweth they were noe names of Welshmen'. He also cites place-names such as Laman's Kiln, Giles' Lake, Hickman's Cross, Harpland, Saiesland, Kadman's Park, Bonteyn's Park, The Slade, Warren Tree Lake, Marlas Knock, Brown's Cliff, Picked Stone, Maggot's Ditch, Carford, Hanging Stone, Sliphill [Sheephill?] and Clerkenwell to 'shew that in auncient tymes the towne was inhabited by the Normans and the Englishe brought thither at the tyme the countrey was first conquered'. These names, he adds, 'for the most parte yett remain, althoughe the people are nowe become meere Welsh in speeche'.

By the fifteenth century a great number of the burgage-holders bore Welsh names: Llewelyn ap Rhys ap Robert, Llewelyn ap Rhys ap Llewelyn ab Owen, Alson ferch Robyn, Gwilym Hir, William Foel, Margaret Llewelyn and Jany Goch figured among the surviving English, or Anglo-Norman, names.

Hickman's Hill may have been the upper part of the Pen-y-bont road, as Hickman's Cross was near the top of that road, with a lane leading off it, past a close called Parc Croes Hickman, to join Lower St Mary Street. Goldsmith Street may have been associated with 'Goldsmithe's burgage' lying in the middle of Mabudrud Street, and Watch Street may have some connection with Cnwc-y-Watch which was also in that vicinity. Street names that are only a memory include Owen's Row, Park Lane, Vaughan's Row and Water Street.

The extent of 1434 lists 233 burgages in the town, and 29 that lay outside it. Long Street had 46 burgages on its west side and 42 on the east. The burgage held by John ap Robert on The Cross, at the corner of Long Street and Bridge Street, was called the Toll-house. He also held three burgages at the opposite corner, together with seven and a half

Aerial view from the north showing St Mary Street and Long Street, and traces of the burgages.

burgages near the bottom of Long Street, two and a half in West Street, two in Goat Street, one in Mabudrud Street, and nine and a half in St Mary Street. Only Jenkin Picton, with thirty nine burgages held more. Thomas Devonald, with sixteen burgages, and Thomas Jordan with thirteen, were the other large burgage-holders. The burgages outside the town included land at Trecadifor, Trewreiddig, Holmhouse, Focl Goch, Castellygarn, Coedcadw, Llystyn Isaf, Brithdir and Y Gamallt.

During excavation carried out by the Dyfed Archaeological Trust on the site of the new school, in the lower part of Long Street, in 1992,[17] the sites of three burgages were uncovered. Each contained a dwelling, built of clay, or clom, which is a mixture of clay and straw, and roofed, probably, with slate tiles. Two of the dwellings were built with their frontage to the street and the other, between them, had its gable end to the road and stood further back from it. They appeared to have been occupied soon after the foundation of the town, and they may have been the burgages shown on the 1434 rent roll in the occupation of Jenkin Picton, Llywelyn ap Rhys ap Robert and John ap Robert. By 1594 they were unoccupied and in the hands of the lord of Cemais.

The extent 'made and renewed' on 26 May 1594[18] 'before Hugh Lewis, gent., mayor of the said town, by perambulation and inquisition of the burgesses and freeholders of the town', listed 211 burgages, of which only 50 were 'in repair' and paying the full rent of 12d (5p) per annum, while the others were 'in decay' and paying only 6d, yielding in all an income of £6.10.6 (£6.52) that year. In addition, rents received for tenements outside the town, including Trecadifor 12d., Holmhouse 3s (15p) and Brithdir 20d (8p), accounted for another 11s.7d (58p). The burgage at

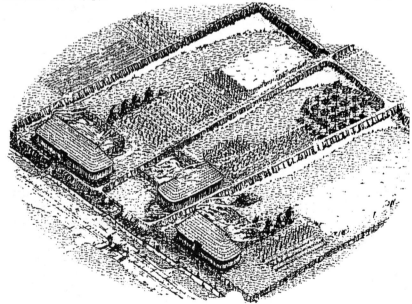

Artist's impression of burgage plots in Long Street excavated by the Dyfed Archaeological Trust in 1991.

the corner of Market Street and Church Street is said to have been 'formerly called le Wollhouse', and opposite was the burgage 'called the old Sheere hall', while 'le Sheere hall formerly called le Tolehouse' stood on The Cross, at the corner of Long Street and Bridge Street. Some fifty yards down Long Street, on the west side, was 'half a burgage called le Jaile'. The estate of the recently deceased Sir John Perrot held no less than 34 burgages, and John Devonald had 31, some of which were held in 1434 by Thomas Devonald, presumably an ancestor. Twenty of the burgages held by John Devonald were in the tenure of Henry Stedman, who lived in 'the big house' half way up Market Street on the east side. He appears to have been a prominent businessman, and was mayor in 1585.

The 'profits of the town'[19] accruing to the lord of Cemais that year, in addition to Burgage rents amounting to £7.2s.1d. (£7.10) comprised 13s.4d. (66p) for the prise of ale, £7.18s.4d. (£7.92) from the Castle Mill, 13s.4d. from the weir, 15s. (75p) from demesne lands, and hen rents to the value of 16d. (7p) making a grand total of £17.3s.5d. (£17.17). The Castle Mill was leased to Lewis David Lloyd for £6.13.4d. (£6.66), to which was added the toll paid by the tenants of the Bury, amounting to 25s. (£1.25). The demesne lands included the half-burgage in Long Street on which the Jail stood, four and a half acres of land at Foel Goch in the parish of Nevern, half acre at Cwm Dewi, and the Castle Park, containing about 6 acres which adjoined the moat on the south side of the castle, and which was also leased to Lewis David Lloyd, the miller, for 5s. (25p), a hen and a day's reaping.

The moat served as a millpond for the Castle mill, and the burgesses were bound by custom to grind their corn there. The other mills, all in decay, were the one that stood near St Milburg's chapel, on or near the site of New Mill; one that 'stood a little above Newport Bridge by St Curig's chapel at a place called in old time Millbrook', and a mill that was near the house at Rhigian.[20] The water that drove that mill had been diverted to drive the nearby mill of Thomas ab Owen.

The rental refers to 'the highway through the middle of the town towards Fishguard',[21] which is not mentioned in earlier rentals, and it has been suggested that it may have been built about this time to replace the previous through road, along Upper West Street, Church Street and Goat Street.

While the rent of a burgage was 12d (5p) per annum, some paid only a nominal charge. The burgage next to Afon Y Felin was held for the rent of half a penny or a red rose paid at Easter, and others were held for a capon, or a fat hen at Shrovetide. The inhabitants of the north side of West Street and of both sides of Cock Lane, except corner houses, paid no rent but did service, including dressing and leading home the hay growing upon the meadows of the Bury and on the Marsh; lead and carry home wood, coal and fuel to the castle; cleanse and repair the mill leet as required, and lead any horse-drawn carriages carrying timber necessary for the repair of the mill. These services were known as *servicia integra,* and fifteen burgages and sixteen half-burgage were charged with their performance.[22]

The rental stated that 'in ancient tyme, when the lordes of the baronye of Kemes dwelled in the castell of Newporte they used the saide landes of Bury as theire demeynes, beinge a peece of grownde very large and very good for corne and sheepe . . . and it standeth so that every parte thereof may be seene owt of the castell of Newporte. When the lordes departed to dwell out of ye countrey then it was first rented owt to the inhabitantes of Newport to till and occupie.'[23] There was also the Burrows, or the Warren comprising about sixty acres of sandy ground which was good for sheep pasture and rabbits, and which the tenants were allowed to graze for no rent, and ' certen hills abowte the saide grownde' called Coed Llonc, that were full of timber in times past but by then denuded, as the burgesses of Newport had estover, or allowance of wood, there. There was also the Sheephill where there was pasture for sheep and a store of furze, comprising about eighty acres that were grazed without payment of rent 'by sufferance'.

The demesne lands at the Bury were divided into six parcels at a rental of £3 6s 8d (£3.33) each.[24] Hugh Lewis, the recorder of Cemais, had one-and-a-half parcels, and he also rented a meadow called Bury's Mead at 13s 4d (66p) per annum, and 'Llonc's Mead *alias* le Marsh' at 11s 8d (58p), a total of 25s (£1.75). The rest of the Bury lands were rented in half, or lesser, portions of a parcel among seventeen other tenants. Each of these also paid one hen at Christmas, each hen being valued at 4d., and Hugh Lewis rendered six capons, worth 6d. each. Each tenant, except Hugh Lewis, had to do a day's harrowing and carry manure for a day, each day being worth 6d., and also do a day's reaping and a day carrying lime to the lord's mansion at Henllys, each worth 4d., the total value of the work amounting to 28s 4d (£1.42). The tenants were bound to grind their corn at the Castle Mill, the toll for which amounted to 25s (£1.25). Lands at the Bury called *Tir y River* and *Tir Kyd*, valued at 3s 4d., were in nobody's tenure, and the cliff quarries were not in use and not set at any value.

The range of the demands upon a tenant are illustrated in the grant of a lease by George Owen, in 1577, of a twelfth part of The Bury to David Meredudd of Newport at an annual rental of 33s.4d.,[25] together with a hen at Shrovetide, a man to help reap the harvest, a man with two horses to lead dung, one day's harrowing, one horse to fetch a load of lime, and one horse to fetch a load of salt or coals. He was also subject to a heriot, namely, a render of the best live beast to the lord on the tenant's death, and *arian ymado*, a payment, or fine, if he left without warning, and he had to undertake to grind all his corn at the Castle Mill

There appears to have been a proposal, in that year, to remove St Meugan's Fair from Eglwyswrw to The Bury, for the lessor is assured that if this should take place, he 'shall have the ground necessary to serve such a fair with all profits'.[26]

THE MAYOR

The first mayor of whom there is record was Richard Suetman who witnessed a charter of Nicholas Martin in about 1278 as *preposito de Novo burgo*.[1] He was the successor in an office that may have been in existence for, perhaps, sixty years, for the charter granted by Nicholas Martin in about 1241,[2] which decreed that 'the burgesses ought to have a reeve and a catchpole appointed by consultation with the lord' of Cemais, was a confirmation of the liberties and customs granted by his father, William Martin, who had died in 1216.

The *prepositus*, reeve or portreeve, as he was variously known until about 1500, after which he is referred to as 'mayor', was chosen by the lord of Cemais from a list of four names of burgesses, including the name of the retiring mayor, submitted to him by a grand inquisition of jurors selected at the Court Leet and View of Frankpledge. He was sworn at the Michaelmas Court where he took an oath 'to well and truly execute and exercise the office of Mayor for the Town and Liberties of Newport within the Barony of Cemais for the ensuing year, ... do equal right to the poor and to the rich, ... take nothing for executing the said office but the accustomed fees, and ... in all things ... well truly justly and honestly do and execute the office of Mayor according to the best of my knowledge and power vested in me'. He was answerable to the lord for rents, tolls, waifs and strays, and estreats and prise of ale which formerly yielded £3 but was now farmed out to him at 13s. 4d. per annum, for him to make what profit he could. He had no salary but received 1s. on the admission of a burgess and, more latterly, the tolls of the two fairs.

The Bailiff was chosen by the Mayor from a list of three, or sometimes four, names submitted to him, which normally included that of the retiring bailiff, and he was sworn by the recorder of the court. It was his duty to serve writs, collect fines and take charge of prisoners. The bailiff appointed in 1629 was given 'a pair of great bolts, two pairs of small bolts with two rings and a shackle'.[3]

The Bailiff was also the Pound Keeper and was entitled to a fine of 2d. for each stray animal released to its owner. In 1834 the Pound (SN 045384) was reported by the mayor, Thomas Owen, to be in need of repair and the necessary work was carried out. It was in use until about 1930, after which it began to fall into decay. A proposal by the author to have it restored, in 1951, was opposed by a burgess who regarded it as a symbol of feudalism and vassalage. It is now maintained as an ancient monument

Four petty constables were appointed and sworn in at the May Court in 1833.[4]

Burgesses were selected from 'fit and proper persons' by the jurors 'by consent of the lord and the reeve' and, after being sworn in open court, they were 'free to enjoye any libertyes within the said towne' as defined in the charter of Nicholas Martin. They held parcels of land, or burgages, for which they paid a rent of 12d. per annum and, sometimes, a fat hen or a capon at Christmas, or a red rose at Easter or upon the Feast of St John the Baptist.

A burgess who misbehaved, or refused to pay his dues, was 'disgraded in the manner he was elected', and he was 'barred from all the liberties and freedom that he enjoyed as a burgess'. William Melchior of Brithdir, who had encroached on the common and built a stone wall 'west of his mansion house and northwards towards Carn Ingli', when ordered to remove it, failed to do so and was deprived of his rights as a burgess.[5]

Following the impeachment of James, Lord Audley, in 1497, the implementation of feudal rights does not appear to have been duly exercised and when the barony was sold to William Owen, in 1543, the new lord complained that the portreeve and burgesses had alienated lands to their own use and, in 1557, he filed a bill at the Council in the Marches against the mayor, Morgan Thomas, and the burgesses, for failing to pay the arrears of rent for the previous four years amounting to £28.[6]

George Owen's right to hold Courts Baron and Courts Leet was subjected to inquiry at the Great Sessions for the county of Pembroke in 1572.[7] The Queen's attorney maintained that the town of Newport was not incorporated, but nothing was done to affect Owen's position, and he also survived a series of *quo warranto* proceedings that were brought against him on the same issue over the next forty years. On each occasion he pleaded that Cemais had been a marcher lordship the lords of which still enjoyed certain privileges, even though lordships marcher had been abolished by the Act of Union. He continued to maintain that Cemais was held of the Crown, even though he himself had recorded that its lords had recognised its jurisdictional dependence upon the earldom of Pembroke since the time of Nicholas Martin. He produced his evidence in lengthy documents, such as his 'Prooffes out of Auntient Recordes, Writings and other matters, that the Lordshipp of Kemes is a Lordshippe marcher,'[8] and, in about 1594, he completed his 'Treatise of Lordshipps Marchers in Wales' which was long regarded as the standard work on the subject.[9]

A marcher lord held a lordship in the March, which was the frontier region between Wales and England. As the king, William I, did not have the resources to conquer the Welsh, he placed his trusted supporters in this border land and made them earls of Hereford, Chester and Shrewsbury. The March reached into the heart of Wales and westward along the south coast to include the Gower peninsula and Pembrokeshire, and it comprised a congeries of some forty lordships. A marcher lord held a unique position in that, in addition to his positon as a Norman baron, he also assumed the regal powers of the Welsh princedom he had conquered. Each lord was a feudal potentate within his own territory, able to build his own castle, create boroughs, institute markets and fairs, hold courts, build prisons and erect his own gallows. He recognised the suzerainty of the king, but the monarch could not interfere in the affairs of the lordship, nor enter except when the lord died without an heir, or was convicted of a felony or treason. Each lordship was held *in capite* of the Crown. When the Act of Union of 1536 created shires that absorbed the marcher lordships, the Lords Marcher lost their judicial powers but retained their seigneurial rights over their tenantry and lands, and were still able to receive rents and dues, and to hold manorial courts.

George Owen complained in 1606[10] that he had lost **more than** £300 in rent, tolls and other dues through the failure, or refusal, of several mayors to collect them. Furthermore, successive mayors and burgesses, had allowed illegal enclosure of commons, the annexation of burgage lands and infringement of the liberties of the town to his detriment. They had been encouraged in their disaffection by the local gentry, prominent among whom were William Warren of Trewern who, nevertheless **was** mayor in 1600, and James Bowen of Llwyngwair, who held the office in 1604.

Owen filed a bill at the Council in the Marches **against** the burgesses for certain irregularities in their method of 'electing a Portreeve (now called a Mayor)'. According to ancient custom, the burgesses were to nominate four of their number from whom the lord appointed one to the office of mayor, 'but good Lords,' he protested to the members of the Council, 'so yt ys now they present only two.' This was a device used by the burgesses to put forward only the names of those who had undertaken not to collect rents and dues. On 26 October 1606 he attended the Court Leet and asked the burgesses to accept the nomination of Hugh Lewis, his trusty lieutenant of many years' standing, who was mayor in 1590-94 and was recorder of the barony, but they refused.

This state of affairs continued for four-and-a-half years, until the townspeople approached him complaining that the trade and welfare of the borough had suffered since the town was without a mayor and corporation, and entreating him to restore the old order. On 16 May 1611, the leading burgesses spent the morning with him, at Henllys, and eventually agreed to his terms. A Court was called that afternoon, at which he was present, and four names were submitted to him, including that of Hugh Lewis, which he chose.

Hugh Lewis was a man of considerable influence in the barony. He was a friend and adviser to George Owen, being about twenty years older, from Owen's youthful days. He is described as 'of Nevern' but nothing is known of his lineage. His later position in society is indicated by his marriage to Mary, daughter of John Philipps of Picton and widow of Mathias Bowen of Llwyngwair, who had died in 1558. He held land of George Owen at Berry Hill in 1594, and Capel Real (St Milburg) of John Bradshaw of St Dogmael's.[11]

Lewis may not have been sworn as mayor at the May meeting, for James Bowen of Llwyngwair presided at the next court,[12] in October, although he may have done so until Lewis was sworn at that meeting. Bowen's grandson, another James Bowen, had his term as mayor broken when his place was taken in August 1661 by Thomas Jones, the mayor of the previous year.

Alban Owen complained to the Council in the Marches in 1638 that the mayor, James Vaughan, had not paid the burgage rents.

On 21 November 1721, Thomas Philipps of Pentre Ifan, who had been previously mayor in 1713, was expelled from office, and John Foley was appointed in his place, and he again was expelled in December 1722, when Thomas Philipps of Rhosmaen, Meline, was appointed. No reason is given for these expulsions but it is noted that they took place around the time of the death of William Owen without issue, when the barony passed to his sisters and coheirs, Elizabeth Laugharne of Llanrheithan and Anne Lloyd of Penpedwast.

At 'a poll for the mayor' at the Court Leet held on 22 October 1759,[13] the discussion became so heated that the mayor, Lewis George David, had to adjourn the Court to the 27th of that month, but again the burgesses could not agree on the nomination and the Court was further adjourned to 1 November when, following 'a declaration of poll', Lewis John William was selected to top the list submitted to Thomas Lloyd, lord of Cemais. The next day, George Bowen of Llwyngwair, as recorder of the barony, wrote to Thomas Lloyd expressing his concern about the method of appointing a mayor.[14] By 1762 the matter had escalated to the extent that there was an 'order in the suit between the King and Lewis John William that George Bowen shall produce the records of the town of Newport for John Stokes, attorney for the King,' to inspect.

At the Court Leet and Court Baron held on 8 May 1812, John Ladd presented 'Lettice Williams, widow, David Salmon, weaver, Thomas Salmon, weaver, John Howell, Nantryw, Evan Rees, Trwchyn, John Rees, Pantry, John Thomas, clothier, David Jenkins, shoemaker, and John James, weaver, being fit and proper persons to be fined for sending their cattle and digging and cutting turf and mats for fire on the mountain of Newport being the property of the Lord of the Manor and Burgesses of Newport.'

At the same court it was presented that David Thomas of Newport, Thomas Williams of Dolrannog and John Jenkin of Parrog be constables for the ensuing year, and also that 'the present Mayor must imidiately procure a Book for the purpose of enrolling the several Presentments which may be found, and it is therefore ordered that any Presentments or Records which may now be in the hands of any Aldermen should be imidiately given up to the present Mayor for the purpose of copying the same, and the same, as well as the Book, to be delivered up to every succeeding Mayor.' The court then stood adjourned, 'to be beholden at the house of Thomas Mathias on Tuesday, the 30th day of June next for the purpose of collecting strayed sheep and cattle.' The jurors present were Thomas Mathias. Mayor; David Thomas, Foreman; Thomas Williams, Dolrannog, Bailiff; Thomas James, Nantyrhedyn; John Ladd, Brithdir Bach; David Harries, shopkeeper; William Thomas, High Street; John Hughes, innkeeper; John Jenkin, Parrog; Stephen Lewis, Tredrysi; Thos Lewis, Cwmdewi; Thomas Rowlands, Nantyblodau; William Beynon, tailor; and William Roberts, shoemaker.

In 1826 the aldermen and burgesses wanted to have Thomas Williams of Dolrannog appointed mayor, but Thomas Lloyd insisted on selecting William Wigley and, for about six months, the town had two mayors, but then Wigley withdrew and Williams remained in office until 1829. Williams appears to have been the subject of dispute again when his name was put forward in 1837, as counsel's opinion was obtained on his appointment, which was deferred.[15] On 31 March 1838 a writ was issued commanding the lord of Cemais, his steward, the late mayor and the burgesses to appoint a mayor, and this was followed, on 8 May, by a mandamus to present three names, one of whom to be mayor. Thomas Williams was appointed for the remainder of the year.[16]

The Mayor, John Harries of Spring Hill, and the Court Leet brought pressure on Thomas Davies Lloyd in 1861 to have a 'Common Council' at Newport, and he instructed his solicitors, Clayton, Cookson and Wainwright to obtain the opinion of Rondell Palmer, QC, who, after noting the character of the charter and of the courts, the privileges enjoyed by the burgesses and the method of appointing the mayor, and the fact that Newport was, and had been for centuries, a corporation, advised against applying to the Queen's bench for a mandamus for the establishment of a Common Council in the town.[17]

Concern for the future of the town was also felt twenty one years later when Sir Marteine Lloyd submitted a petition to the Lords Spiritual and Temporal pleading for the retention of the ancient privileges of the borough of Newport.[18]

Levi Griffiths, of Mauritius, was installed mayor in November 1899 in the absence of Sir Marteine Lloyd by the deputy mayor, John Williams, Cross House, chemist, who had been the mayor in 1865-67, supported by the Steward, David Davies, Solicitor, Cardigan.[19] Griffiths succeeded Captain William Davies, Commercial Hotel, who had established the Town and Parrog Improvements Fund. His successor was Captain John Meyrick, of Mount Pleasant, who must have been one of the oldest to be appointed to the office at the age of 86 years. He died within two months of being installed and his place was taken by John Williams.

Captain David Mathias, installed in 1905, had as one of his first duties the admission of John Wynford Philipps, later Viscount St David's, and Martin Kemes Arundel Lloyd, Sir Marteine's son and heir, as burgesses.[20] Captain Mathias, soon after his installation, was sworn as a magistrate 'after the manner of his predecessors.' A report in a supplement to the *Haverfordwest and Milford Haven Telegraph* of 18 July 1860, stated that 'the Mayor of Newport is recognised in all cases as a Magistrate holding the Queen's Commission. He qualifies in Quarter Sessions, his name is called over at the Assizes with the other magistrates of the County, and he sits as Chief Magistrate in the Borough of Newport.'

At the mayoral banquet following the installation of Captain Mathias in 1906, an attempt to introduce politics during the post-prandial speeches was 'ruled out of order and the speaker was asked to sit down.'[21]

Flags and bunting were flown from buildings along the streets of the town in October 1900 to mark the coming-of-age of Nesta, the eldest daughter of Sir Marteine and Lady Lloyd.[22] The church bells were rung, a huge bonfire was lit on the summit of Carn Ingli, and a firework display was given on The Cross.

Early one Sunday morning in August 1934, a small aeroplane crashed into the mountainside below Carn Ingli. Its occupants were Lieutenant George Pond, of the United States Army Air Force, and Captain Cesare Sabelli, and they had left Rome in their aircraft, named *Leonardo da Vinci*, for Dublin on their return trip to New York. They had made a miraculous escape and had been able to walk away from the plane. They were well entertained by the townspeople, and by Lady Lloyd at the Castle, and Sabelli, who stayed on for some weeks after Pond had departed, was received by the Mayor, Aldermen and Burgesses at a Court Leet.

The Mayor and Corporation with Lady Lloyd and Captain Cesare Sabelli whose aeroplane crashed at Newport, August 1934.

When the author was installed Mayor in 1950, he presented the Lady Marcher, Morfa Withington, with a red rose. It had been the custom, in former days, for burgages to be held for the rent of a red rose rendered on the Feast of St John the Baptist, and Kemes Lloyd, mindful of this custom, used to send his mother, Lady Lloyd, a red rose on her birthday. When he was serving in France during the Great War, he could not find a rose but, instead, he sent her a red flower that grew on the field of battle, which later became widely known as the Flanders Poppy. The gesture has been continued by succeeding mayors.

The mayor's chain was presented to 'the Mayor and Corporation of Newport, Pembrokeshire, by Martin Kemes Arundel Lloyd of Bronwydd on the occasion of his first visit to the ancient borough, 1896', and the medallion by his sisters in the following year 'to commemorate the sixtieth anniversary of the accession of Her Majesty Queen Victoria, 1897'. The badge and chain for the Mayoress was presented to commemorate the Festival of Britain the opening of which in London was attended by the Mayor and Mayoress in 1951.

Newport had its first royal visit in 1951 when HRH Princess Marina, Duchess of Kent, was received by the Mayor before a large gathering of townspeople on a dais erected in Market Street, above The Cross, during her tour of south-west Wales.

Little is known of the early portreeves, or mayors, but there may be a reference to a fifteenth century holder of the office in a poem addressed by Deio ab Ieuan Ddu to Thomas Andrew requesting a pair of swans as a gift for Ieuan ap Siencyn Llwyd of Llwyndafydd in Ceredigion.[23] The poet praises him for his hospitality, his well-laden table, the 'metheglin

The Mayor presenting a red rose to the Lady Marcher.

Royal visit: HRH Princess Marina, Duchess of Kent, July 1951.

and desserts, and wines from France for the young bards'. He is 'a lion among men' and his praise is sung throughout Cemais and, as he has 'the government of Trefdraeth' in his hands, it is reasonable to assume that he was the mayor in about 1480.

During the seventeenth and the early part of the eighteenth century the office of mayor was held by some of the leading gentlemen of the locality. They included William Warren of Trewern (1600-01), James Bowen of Llwyngwair (1604-05 and 1611-13), Thomas Warren of Trewern (1619-20 and 1624-25), James Vaughan of Pontfaen (1629-30 and 1631-33), Henry Philipps of Pentre Ifan (1630-31), William Griffith of Penybenglog (1655-56), Owen Wogan of Llanstinan (1661-63), Thomas Corbet of Wenallt and Nash (1680-81), John Ford of Berry Hill (1709-10), Thomas Knolles of Nevern (1710-11), George Lewes of Hendre, Meline (1711-12), John Colby of Rhosygilwen (1726-27) and Thomas Lloyd of Cwmgloyn (1732-33). Thereafter and throughout the nineteenth century the mayors were selected from the ranks of the townspeople and included master mariners, surgeons, clergy and ministers, drapers, a chemist, a hotelier and a major-general. During the twentieth century with the exception of Sir George Bevan Bowen of Llwyngwair (1913-14) and Sir Evan D Jones, Bart., of Pentower. Fishguard, the mayors have been gentlemen from a wide range of professions.

The following is a list of recorded mayors:

1275	Richard Suetman.
1281	David Ros.
1378	Ieuan ap Waryn.
1390	John Gwrda.
1391	David Lloyd.

1392	David ap Walter.
1393	John Goch.
1394	Thomas Devonald.
1395	William ab Ieuan ap Howel.
1397	Howel ap Richard.
1424	Walter Mendus.
1434	John Picton.
c.1480	Thomas Andrew.
1484	John Lapp.
1485	Llywelyn ap David ab Ieuan Ddu.
1503	William Mendus.
1504	David Robert.
1512	Rees Wall'e.
1553-7	Morgan Thomas.
1585	Henry Stedman.
1588-90	Lewis Philipps, Pentre Ifan.
1590-94	Hugh Lewis, Nevern.
1600-01	William Warren, Trewern.
1601-04	Rees Lloyd.
1604-05	James Bowen, Llwyngwair.
1605-06	Rees Lloyd.
1611-12	Hugh Lewis, Nevern.
1612-13	James Bowen, Llwyngwair.
1613-14	William Davies.
1614-16	Rees Lloyd.
1616-17	John Vaughan.
1619-21	Thomas Warren, Trewern.
1621-23	Owen Picton, Nevern.
1624-25	Thomas Warren, Trewern.
1625-26	George Bowen, Nevern.
1626-28	David ap David.
1628-29	Henry Melchior, Brithdir.
1629-30	James Vaughan, Pontfàen.
1630-31	Henry Philipps, Pentre Ifan.
1631-33	James Vaughan, Pontfaen.
1633-34	George Gwyn.
1635-36	John Vaughan.
1636-37	David ap David.
1637-38	James Vaughan.
1638-39	Thomas Jones.
1639-40	Thomas Griffith.
1640-52	George Bowen, Llwyngwair.
1653-55	Alban Warren, Trewern.
1655-56	William Griffith, Penybenglog.
1658-59	Thomas Jones, Alderman.
1660-61	James Bowen, Llwyngwair.
	Thomas Jones (from August 1661).
1661-63	Owen Wogan, Llanstinan.
1663-64	Thomas Jones.
1664-66	Thomas Griffiths.
1666-69	Alban Warren, Trewern.
1669-72	William Owen.
1672-75	Alban Warren, Trewern.
1675-77	Thomas Johnes.
1677-79	Thomas Griffiths.

1679-80	Richard Lewis.
1680-81	Thomas Corbett, Wenallt and Nash.
1682-84	Thomas Jones, Wenallt.
1684-89	Roger Philipps, Rhosmaen, Meline.
1709-10	John Ford, Berry Hill.
1710-11	Thomas Knolles, Wenallt.
1711-12	George Lewes, Hendre.
1712-13	John Philipps.
1713-21	Thomas Philipps, Pentre Ifan (expelled 21 November, 1721).
1721-22	John Foley (expelled 17 December, 1722).
1722-24	Thomas Philipps, Rhosmaen, Meline.
1724-25	James Bowen.
1725-26	Robert Griffith, Penybenglog.
1726-27	John Colby, Rhosygilwen.
1727-28	Thomas Lloyd.
1729-30	John Thomas.
1730-32	Thomas Lewis.
1732-33	Thomas Lloyd, Cwmgloyn.
1734-35	David Rosser.
1736-37	Thomas Davids.
1738-40	Thomas Lewis.
1740-41	David Rosser.
1741-42	David Harry.
1743-44	Thomas Rees.
1744-45	Evan Rees.
1745-46	David Davies.
1747-48	John Phillips.
1748-49	Evan Rees.
1749-50	James Bateman.
1750-51	David Davies.
1752-53	Thomas Rees.
1753-54	John James.
1754-55	Evan Rees.
1755-56	Thomas Rees.
1756-57	David Davies.
1757-58	Owen Havard, Pendre.
1758-59	Lewis George alias Lewis David.
1759-60	Lewis John William.
1760-61	Thomas Henton the elder.
1761-62	John Griffiths.
1762-63	John James.
1763-64	John Griffiths.
1764-66	John James.
1767-68	Thomas Rees.
1768-69	John James.
1770-71	Lewis Rees.
1771-72	John Lloyd.
1772-74	John James.
1774-76	John Lloyd.
1776-77	Lewis Rees.
1777-78	William Owen.
1778-79	John James.
1779-80	William Owen.
1780-81	Lewis Rees.

1781-82	David Davies.
1782-84	Jacob Picton.
1784-87	David Davies.
1787-88	James Bowen, Llwyngwair.
1788-90	Thomas Morgan.
1790-92	Thomas Mathias.
1792-1801	John Ladd.
1803	Thomas Mathias.
1807	Daniel Thomas.
1812-21	Thomas Mathias.
1822	Thomas Devonald.
1823	John Meyrick.
1824-25	John Owen.
1825-26	Daniel Evans.
1826-28	Thomas William, Dolrannog (nominated by the Court Leet). William Wigley (appointed by the Lord)
1829-30	William Llewellyn.
1830-31	David Davies.
1831-32	William Llewellyn.
1832-33	Stephen Owen.
1833-34	John Owen.
1834-35	David Hughes, Parciau.
1835-36	John Hughes.
1836-37	John Evans.
1837-38	Thomas Williams.
1838-41	Edward Rees.
1841-43	John Hughes.
1843-45	Thomas Harries, retired master mariner.
1845-50	John Harries.
1850-51	Levi Havard.
1851-52	William Evans, retired master mariner.
1852-53	Thomas Owen Bevan, surgeon.
1853-55	John Llewellyn, surgeon.
1855-57	Rev. Ll. Ll. Thomas, rector.
1857-58	Rev. Samuel Thomas, Congregational Minister.
1858-61	William Williams, Parciau.
1861-63	John Harries, Spring Hill.
1863-65	David Seaborne, draper.
1865-67	John Williams, Cross House, chemist.
1867-69	John Harries.
1869-70	Rev. James Jenkins, Baptist minister.
1870-72	James Bevan Bowen, M.P., Llwyngwair.
1872-74	Rev. David George, Baptist minister.
1874-76	Rev. J. G. Morris, Congregational Minister.
1876-78	David Havard, M.D., East View.
1878-80	Capt. William Evans, Cross House.
1880-82	William Rees, Spring Hill.
1882-84	David Price Jones, Upper West Street, draper.
1884-86	Rev. James Jenkins, Baptist Minister.
1886-88	Rev. George Morgan, Methodist Minister.
1888-90	Stephen Evans, Fountain House.
1890-91	Thomas James Davies.
1893-95	Major-General Charles Sturt, Newport Castle.
1895-97	John Hughes, Pendre.

1897-98	Dr. H. Bowen Perkins, Llysmeddyg.
1898-99	Captain William Davies, Commercial Hotel.
1899-1901	Levi Griffiths, Mauritius.
1901-02	Captain John Meyrick, Mount Pleasant.
1902-04	John Williams, Cross House.
1904-06	Henry Rees Felix, Bridge House.
1906-08	Captain David Mathias.
1908-10	Captain David Jones, Ivy House.
1910-11	Rev. David Jones Evans, Baptist minister.
1911-13	Captain John Davies
1913-14	Sir George Bevan Bowen, Llwyngwair.
1914-16	Canon D. G. Phillips, rector.
1916-17	Sir Evan D. Jones, Bart., Pentower, Fishguard.
1917-20	Dr. David Havard, East View.
1920-22	James Oliver Vaughan, Dewi Villa.
1922-23	Frederick Edward Withington, Bicester.
1923-25	David Thomas, Swn-y-Don.
1925-27	David Luke, New Mill.
1927-29	John Llewellyn Havard, East Street.
1929-31	Thomas Williams, Maescynon.
1931-33	Canon Glynfab Williams, Rector of Dinas.
1933-35	Caleb Morris, Tan-y-bryn.
1935-37	John Bowen Evans, Llys Dewi.
1937-39	John R. Harries, Trewarren.
1939-41	Benjamin Williams, Llwyngwair Arms.
1941-43	David Howard Roberts, Delfan.
1943-45	Ebenezer Richard Gronow, Lyndale.
1945-46	Rev. Jeffrey Jones, Rector.
1946-48	Thomas Harries Vaughan, Commercial Hotel.
1948-50	William Morgan Jermain, Mount Pleasant.
1950-51	Dillwyn Miles, Newport Castle.
1951-53	John Owen, Cnwce.
1953-54	Rev. John Jenkins, Rector.
1954-56	Rev. L. G. Lewis, Baptist Minister.
1956-58	George J. T. Evans, Bro Dawel.
1958-60	William Lewis Williams, Ffynnonddofn.
1960-62	J. Clayton Thatcher, Craig-y-mor.
1962-64	Dr. D. M. Lodwick Evans.
1964-66	Morton Tucker, Major House.
1966-68	Dillwyn Miles.
1968-70	Rev. Eric Williams.
1970-72	J. Clayton Thatcher.
1972-74	Captain Morris John Morgan.
1974-76	Dr. J. C. Bignall.
1976-77	Rev. M. M. Griffiths, Rector.
1977-79	Barry John.
1979-80	Dillwyn Miles.
1980-82	Glyn Rees.
1982-84	Robin Evans.
1984-86	Elwyn John.
1986-88	Rev. Granville Varney.
1988-90	Ewart Daniel.
1990-91	Dr. Anthony Clark.
1991-94	Lawrence Varney.
1994-	Rev. R. C. Jones, Rector.

LAW AND ORDER

Among the 'prooffes that Kemes is an aunciente lordshippe marcher' advanced by George Owen was his claim that the lord of Cemais had *jura regalia,* that is, power of life and death, within the lordship; that he had 'a gaole for ffelons in his castle', a gallows for 'the executinge of ffelons', and a constable of his castle 'whose office was to keepe the gaole and execute prisoners condempned.'

The gallows stood 'betweene the towne and Cappel Dewy, . . . and the toompe where it stoode is called by the inhabitants Knwc y Krogwith', Owen added. He maintained that 'the hooles where the tree was fastened in the ground is yett very apparaunte' and pointed out that the old name for the site was 'the Warren Tree, which is the proper name of a gallowes among the Englishmen of Pembrokeshire'. The stream that runs by Cnwc y Grogwydd, which was at the junction of the road to Fishguard and the Penfeidr road, is described in 1434 as *Warentrelak*, and Owen refers to it as Warren Tree Lake. The word 'lake' is used in south Pembrokeshire to signify a stream and, in Newport, Afon Ysgolheigion was formerly known as Gilles Lake.

The gaol[2] had been removed from the castle by the end of the sixteenth century and was situate in the fourth burgage down Long Street on the west side, but it was not fit for use by the beginning of the eighteenth century as the Grand Jury, at the Court Leet held on 25 September 1713 presented that a gaol, and a town hall, be built in the town 'upon the charge of the lords of the borough with the benevolences of the burgesses in the place where it was formerly near The Cross'. Other forms of punishment included the stocks and the whipping post which the jury, at the court held on 20 October 1720, reported to be out of repair.

Two courts were held in the borough: the Court Baron, and the Court Leet and View of Frankpledge, the records of which have survived, with a number of gaps, since 1588. Earlier records show that the lord of Cemais administered the law within, or even in excess, of the powers that he held by agreement with the Earl of Pembroke, and, sometimes, he was charged with failing to do so. In 1274 Nicholas Martin complained that the Steward of Pembroke 'did unjustly demaunde of him and his men of Newporte Cs. [100s] for the supposed flyinge and escape of a theeffe called Madog ap Goylchla' who, having been apprehended of theft, escaped from Newport.[3] He had subsequently been 'taken and brought to the castle of Pembroke and for the same felony condemned and hanged'. The Steward claimed that it was a negligent escape because the lord of Cemais had the custody of thieves only for three nights, after which they had to be delivered to Pembroke. This thief had been held for four nights and had not been delivered 'in the due houre' and even though he had been convicted and hanged, the fine still stood.

In 1317 David Sanc, constable of the castle of Newport, appeared before the Sheriff of the county of Pembroke for having taken a reward of a thief and suffered him to escape.[4] He pleaded not guilty but when he saw a jury ready to be sworn, he changed his plea and was fined 40s. He appeared again in the following year, but before the Steward this time, charged with having caused the body of an infant to be buried 'neare

Newport towards the sea' without view of the coroner of Pembroke. His plea was that he had done so because the coroner lived a long way away and that the body had lain there for some time, to the knowledge of the neighbours. He was fined 20s.

In the same year, Madoc ap Sais and Llywelyn ab Owen were indicted for feloniously stealing a jacket worth 20d. and, having fled, their goods and chattels at Newport, valued at 8s.9d. were forfeit to the Earl of Pembroke. Three years later, Madoc ap Sais appeared as 'constable of Newport' when he was fined 3s. 4d. for an escape. In that same year William Martin, lord of Cemais, became pledge for Llywelyn Ddu of Newport who had fled after committing a theft, to the value of 6s.8d.

The courts were held at 'the olde Sheere Hall', at the corner of Market Street and Upper Bridge Street up to the sixteenth century, by which time 'le sheere hall formerly called le Tolehouse' stood at the corner of Long Street and Bridge Street.[5] By about 1625, however, they met at the house of the bailiff and, sometimes, at the mayor's house. During the latter part of the last century, the courts were combined as the Court Leet and Court Baron, and continue so to meet at the Llwyngwair Arms Hotel.

The Court Leet and View of Frankpledge was held twice year, in the spring and around Michaelmas, before the mayor. Burgesses and freeholders, who held land in the parish, owed suit of court and were summoned by warrant 'to make their appearance and attend', and their names were called from a roll by the clerk, or recorder, of the court. If any suitor failed to attend without essoin, that is, a reasonable excuse, he was amerced, or fined, seven shillings. The early records show that there were some seventy to eighty burgesses, and twenty to thirty freeholders.

The mayor selected up to nineteen suitors to form 'a grand inquisition', or jury, 'to inquire for the king and the lord of the manor of the Corporation and Town of Newport' and to make presentments and to amerce offenders. They appointed a Foreman, who was sworn in the court, and the other jurors were then sworn to 'take the like oath' in batches of three at a time.

The View of Frankpledge derived from the Saxon custom of collective responsibility under which one member of a tithing of ten men was bound to stand security for the good behaviour of the others.

Dr B G Charles has selected extracts from the court rolls that will 'give a good idea of this aspect of the business of the Court Leet and View of Frankpledge',[6] among which are the following presentments:

20 April 1589. That Eynon Phillips, gent., died seised as a burgess of the town, wherefore there falls due to the lord, 12d.

3 May 1604. That James Perrot, knight, Walter Rees, knight, Cicil, daughter of James Perrott, Owen Picton, gent., John Kiblewhite and Rowland Thomas Young the Younger, freehold tenants of the town, because they did not appear at the Court of View of Frankpledge but defaulted, are amerced 7s each.

8 October 1604. That Lewis ap Hugh of Haverfordwest and his wife intruded on the liberties of the town and broke the assize of ale there, therefore in mercy 7s.

25 August 1606. That Richard ab Ievan, tailor, and ten others kept taverns in their houses and sold ale without licence.

7 October 1611. Thomas Phillip Gwrda was amerced 40s. by the mayor because he, being present in court, refused to take the oath in evidence on behalf of the king, although desired to do so by the mayor.

12 October 1612. That the highway within the liberty of the town near Park-y-marys is ruinous and in decay.

23 April 1621. The jury present William Anthony, Katherine James, John Lloyd, clerk, and Trevor Hugh, clerk, for keeping mangy horses contrary to the statute, amerced 7s. each.

25 February 1655. Because Thomas Owen Smith did take tobacco in open court he was amerced 3s6d.

The Court Baron, or Hundred Court, upheld the customs of the manor and maintained the rights of the lord against his tenants, and the privileges of the tenants against the lord. It was held every other Monday before the mayor to hear 'pleas of any action personal or mixed of what sum soever, and to the said Court are all freeholders by tenure of their land and burgesses by reason of their freedom bound to do suit and service'. The Bailiff summoned twelve burgesses on a warrant from the mayor to attend the Court, out of whom six were sworn to sit in judgement, and one of them was appointed Foreman, who declared the verdict.

The normal business of the Court Baron was the trial of pleas of debt and detinue, that is, wrongful detention of personal chattels, trespass and slander. Litigants sometimes employed attorneys, who were usually local gentlemen who had received some legal training and who normally charged a fee of 1s.4d. Among them was William Bowen of Holmhouse, a son of Llwyngwair, who, at a court held in March 1613 had his papers snatched and torn to pieces by the irascible William Gwyn of Trericert, who was appearing for the other side. Some of the litigants were merchants and traders from Haverfordwest and elsewhere, or farmers from outside Cemais who were attending the fair.

Examples of cases[7] chosen for illustration by Dr. Charles included:

24 February 1589. Owen Lewys pleaded against George Gwrda, Ellen ferch David and Thomas Gwrda, in a plea of trespass to the damage of plaintiff 10s. made at 'le Westreat in the hagard of plaintiff with the sheep and cattle of the defendant'.

13 September 1590. Rees ab Ievan ap Howell complained against Philip William, pedlar, in a plea of debt 55s.8d. for cheese and butter sold to him on the feast of Phillip and James.

22 July 1611. William Bowen of Hollmus, gent, complained against Gwenllian Ievan, spinster, who had withdrawn her service before the end of the term agreed.

19 August 1611. Alban Owen, gent, claimed 40s. against Thomas Philip Gwrda for not hay-making and leading hay from 'the meadow called Castlemead'.

11 May 1612. Owen John David complained that Griffith ab Ievan Gall, on 1 September 1611, demised 35 sheep to plaintiff to enjoy

their milk and half their wool but had taken the sheep home on 1 May.

31 July 1615. Robert Llewelyn of Fishguard claimed £100 damages against Henry William who, on the High Cross at Newport, had spoken the following scandalous words: 'Lleidr wyt ti a mab i leidr . . . nas gadewaist ti ddim eriod heb ei ddwyn ond a fai rhy drwm neu rhy boeth . . . a mab i leidr sy'n . . . dwyn ceffylau ac yn eu cuddio yn yr eithin' (You are a thief and the son of a thief . . . that never left anything without stealing it, unless it was too heavy or too hot . . . and the son of a thief who steals horses and hides them in the gorse).

One of the most sensational events that ever took place at Newport occurred on 16 June 1578 at Ffair Gurig, when John Jones of Trecwn, a former coroner of the county of Pembroke, was 'very shamfully and horribly murdered by one James Bowen, gentleman, Gryffyn James alias Philipps, John James alias Philipps, both of Pentypark, Thomas Bowen, Henry Bowen and others'.[8] The Bowens were the sons of Mathias Bowen, the first of that family to settle at Llwyngwair, and his wife, Mary, daughter of John Philipps, younger son of Sir Thomas Philipps of Picton. The victim was the brother of Owen Johns of Trecwn, who was married to George Owen's sister.

An action for murder was brought against the defendants and an inquisition was taken before Lewis Powell, gent, of Green Hill, who found that the defendants, 'not having God before their eies, but devellishely ledd and of their mallice before thought . . . did assault John Jones.' Gryffyn Philipps, with his sword held in his right hand, had struck Jones in his breast giving him a wound, 'one inch in width and seven inches deep', from which he died. Philipps was sentenced to death and was duly executed. The others were charged with feloniously abetting, procuring, comforting and helping Gryffyn Philipps, but they were pardoned and, under the statute of 1336, they were required to provide sureties for their subsequent good behaviour. James Bowen, 'beinge a verie subtile, lewd and wicked person', did not do so and gave, as an excuse, that he had been pressed to serve as a soldier on a ship commanded by Sir John Perrot for the defence of Ireland, but this was thought to have been a ruse on the part of Perrot to embarrass George Owen who had taken part in bringing the miscreants to justice. Owen alleged that Bowen had conspired with William Gwyn of Trericert to forge a bond whereby certain gentlemen became bound to the Queen in £100 for his good behaviour, and that Gwyn had forged the signature of the sheriff, Thomas Revell of Forest, Cilgerran, and of Lewis Powell and Ievan Williams of Manorowen, the coroners. Gwyn, in his defence, stated that he had been commissioned to take to Westminster the return of the writ directed to the sheriff, and that he had been authorised by the sheriff and the coroners to affix their names to the bond. When he arrived in London, he had met the defendant, James Bowen, who had told him that the delay in providing recognizance was not his fault as the Queen had appointed 'the Right Worshippful Sir John Perrot, Knight, to be generall of Her Majestie's Navye, then appointed to goe to seas for Her Majestie's service' and he had been pressed as a soldier to go with him until he returned to this country, in October 1579.

Throughout this time Gwyn, along with his father-in-law, Eynon Philipps, were conspiring against George Owen in a number of ways. They challenged his right to wardship of heirs during nonage; they endeavoured to persuade the current Lord Audley that he was the rightful heir to the lordship of Cemais, and they charged Owen with the forgery of documents. The spectre of Owen's arch-enemy, Sir John Perrot, appears behind most, if not all, of these hostile acts, and it was at his instigation that Gwyn was motivated to report Owen to the Lords of the Privy Council, who ordered his arrest.

Owen was arrested, at eleven o'clock on the morning of 26 November 1579, while sitting at his own court at Newport, on a warrant issued by the sheriff, Thomas Revell. He was charged with 'counterfeyting of the greate seale of armes of William, Erle of Pembroke, first of that name, as also for forging certen deedes, etc., to the greate prejudice of the free holders of the lordship of Kaymise.' The warrant was issued to a commission comprising John Barlow of Slebech, John Wogan of Boulston, Morgan Philipps of Picton and Eynon Philipps, of Tregybi, Cardigan, who also had a house at Newport. The sheriff and the commissioners were all known enemies of George Owen, except for Barlow, and he was away at the time. They were required to search for the alleged forgeries and to examine witnesses produced by William Gwyn.

Owen was placed in the custody of two of the high constables of Cemais, who were armed with swords and daggers, while the sheriff and the commissioners leisurely enjoyed a mid-day meal in a local hostelry. They then set off for Henllys, escorted by about thirty person, variously armed, and they arrived there after nightfall. They ransacked the house, looking every where for the alleged forgeries and, in doing so, they damaged the seal of the statute staple for £600 which Lord Audley had handed to William Owen. They found nothing to prove the charge, which infuriated Gwyn, who tried to steal one of the title deeds by concealing it under his cloak. Owen maintained that his wife had suffered a miscarriage on account of the disturbance, but this was not so, for she was delivered of a boy child, Alban, the following July.

The commissioners took away two exemplifications, 'the charter of Pembroke' bearing the date 16 January 1378 under 'the greate seale of England in greene waxe', and the recovery for the lordship of Cemais dated 7 March 1524 'under the chauncery seale of Pembroke in yellow waxe'. They retired to Eynon Philipp's house at Newport to inspect the documents, but could find no fault with them. Gwyn felt thwarted and swore that he would find some other way of discomfitting the lord of Cemais.

The next morning Owen was handed over to the sheriff. He complained that he was kept a prisoner for eighteen days and had been twice taken to Haverfordwest to be made 'a wonder to the countrey', and there forced to remain with his men and horses for six days at his own charge, but Revell maintained that he had kept him at his own house at Cilgerran and had allowed him access to Henllys. Owen appeared before the Privy Council in January 1580, when their lordships dismissed the case from the Council Board and referred it to the Star Chamber, but there is no record of its appearance there.

George Owen was sheriff of the county of Pembroke in 1587 and, again, in 1602.[9] During that year he had the unpleasant duty of arranging the execution of John Bowen and Hugh Bowen, the sons of James Bowen of Llwyngwair, who had killed their cousin, Thomas Young of Tredrysi, in a brawl at Eglwyswrw fair on Ascension Day, 13 May. The extreme penalty was carried out at Haverfordwest on 18 July, and the two brothers were buried in St Mary's churchyard in that town on the same day.[10]

James Bowen's relationship with the lord of Cemais was sufficiently unimpaired for him to be appointed mayor of Newport two years later, and also in 1611.[11] In 1624, when he was nearly eighty years of age, he was appointed sheriff.

Following the death of Alban Owen, lord of Cemais, his successors did not display the same zeal in endeavouring to establish their feudal rights. The people of Newport revealed again their aversion to contributing the accustomed dues when, in 1833, they refused to pay their quit rents to Thomas Lloyd of Bronwydd, lord of Cemais. In the following year, a proclamation, that was said to have been sponsored by George Bowen of Llwyngwair, was issued announcing that persons 'having possessions or erections on the common at Newport need not pay rent to the lord, or to the mayor'.[12]

Newport was never able to acquire the status of a municipal borough, but an attempt was made to include the town in a parliamentary borough in the Reform Act of 1832. In the first draft of the Bill it was added to Fishguard and Narberth as contributory to the Haverfordwest Borough constituency, but it was omitted from the final draft.[13] Its failure to achieve autonomous incorporation was said to be due to its poverty and low population. The report of James Booth, one of the commissioners on Municipal Corporations in England and Wales, which he signed on 30 December 1833, stated that the town had 'no share in the return of a Member of Parliament'.[14]

The report states that the members of the corporation of the borough of Newport 'are a mayor, a bailiff and an indefinite number of aldermen and burgesses'. It gave the number of burgesses as 'about 420', which seems to have been a high proportion of the male population of 708, and confirmed that they were entitled to common of pasture and exemption from tolls, the cutting of turf and 'getting stone from the quarries within the waste [of the manor] but their right to exercise this privilege is disputed by the lord of the borough'.

The corporation of Newport was saved from dissolution in 1883 by the intervention of William Davies, the Liberal Member of Parliament for the county of Pembroke who had succeeded the Tory member, James Bevan Bowen of Llwyngwair.[15] The Municipal Corporations Act of that year stated that 'nothing in this Act shall be deemed to prevent the election of the Mayor of Newport (Pembroke) as heretofore, or to dissolve the corporation of Newport (Pembroke), or deprive the lord of the Manor or the Burgesses of any tolls, rights of common, or other rights of a pecuniary value'.

Following the establishment of Parish Councils by the Local Government Act of 1894, the Newport Parish Council was elected that year, with the Reverend J. G. Morris, minister of Ebenezer Chapel, as its first chairman. Its place was taken, when the Local Government Act of 1972 abolished rural parishes, by the Newport Community Council.

The Representation of the People's Act 1948 decreed that mayors, hitherto appointed in November, should henceforth be installed in April or May, but the Court Leet was persuaded that the Act did not apply in the case of the Mayor of Newport and he, consequently, shares the distinction with the Lord Mayor of London of being the only civic heads still appointed to office in November each year. The election, in each case, originally took place on the feast of St Simon and St Jude, the 28th of October, until the adoption of the Gregorian calendar when the date was changed to 9 November.

The Commission appointed under the Law Commissions Act of 1965[16] for the purpose of reforming the law relating to local courts of special jurisdiction regarded 'the Courts Leet and Baron of the Barony of Cemais' as courts possessing 'non-judicial functions which are still exercised, which are valued locally, and which it was desired to maintain', and recommended that they should be specifically preserved for the exercise of those functions, which were given as 'the taking of presentments with respect to matters of local concern, and the management of the common lands on the Presely Hills'.

The Court Leet and Court Baron still meets twice a year, in May and September, and aldermen and burgesses are summoned by warrant 'to make their appearance and attend', but they are no longer amerced seven shillings for failing to do so. A third court takes place in November for the installation of the mayor, and, since 1964, a special court is held towards the end of August following the perambulation of the boundaries, and this court is open to the public to attend.

The custom of perambulating the boundaries of a parish is said to date from the fifth century when the incidence of plague and tempest prompted the Bishop of Vienna to lead a procession chanting litanies and imploring divine protection on the three Rogation Days preceding Ascension Day. The custom continued with the parish priest being followed by the parishioners and children, all carrying white willow wands bedecked with the rogation flower, the milkwort,and ribbons. The procession halted at boundary marks where small boys were beaten so that they would always remember where the boundaries lay, and they were afterwards rewarded with cakes and sweetmeats. The processions were discontinued as religious observances at the Reformation but they survived as Gang Days, so called from the custom of 'ganging' (going) round the country 'beating the parish bounds'.

There are records[17] of the courts receiving reports of the perambulation of the boundaries of the barony taking place every seven years from 1777 onward. An account of the ceremony held in July 1860 appeared in a supplement to the *Haverfordwest and Milford Haven Telegraph:*

PERAMBULATION OF CEMAES
Wednesday, 11th July 1860:
Assembly at Eglwyswrw, 10am. Mr. & Mrs. Thos. Davies Lloyd and

their young son, Marteine, arrived from the east. A procession was formed:—

The Bronwydd Band; with the flag of the Barony.
Horsed Freeholders of Cemaes;
Mr. T. Lloyd on horseback, with Marteine on a pony;
Mrs. Lloyd in a carriage;
Other vehicles;
The general public, bearing a hundred banners many of which bore Welsh proverbs and mottoes, etc., e.g. "Nor symud yr hen derfyn", "Uwch pen na dwy ysgwydd", "Ni roddir gwlad i fud", "Cas gwr na charo'r wlad a'i maco", "Gwir yn erbyn y byd" etc. One bore "Rhydd-dalwyr Cemaes i'r Baron XXIV".

The procession, numbering over 3000, left Eglwyswrw for Mountain Hall, near Brynberian, where the Baronial Court is by ancient custom opened. Here a Jury of 16 freeholders was sworn in. The procession then divided, some taking the road to Tafarn Bwlch, while the Jury and others struck out across open ground to follow the boundary. Soon an obstruction was found. A dwelling had been built which encroached upon the Common. The occupant turned obstinate and refused entry to the Jury, whereupon the Flag of the Barony was driven through a window, followed by the Bearer and Jury.

At Tafarn Bwlch the two cavalcades were re-united. Foot-followers climbed the hill to Bwlch Gwynt. The horsemen perambulated the North and West boundaries past Tyrbwlch, Trefach, Brynhyfryd, Tygwyn, Wauntralwm, and on to Via Flandrica skirting Foel Erw to the top of Bwlch Gwynt, where they rested and feasted. Then, still skirting Via Flandrica, past Cwm Cerwyn, Ffynnonyrchain, Cerrig Marchogion and Bwlchtreselly. Down the eastern slopes of Bwlchgwynt and Presely to Bedd Arthur, Moel Trigarn, in the valley below which the first day's perambulation concluded amid cheers for Mr. Lloyd, the brattle of the trumpet and waving of banners.

Thursday, 12th July, 1860:
The perambulation resumed early in the morning in the gorge where they had dispersed the previous evening. Then over the crest of Maenllwydyrhos and down to Croes Mihangel. Thence along the north side of the mountain, passing Mynydd Bach, Ffynnonhyfyd, Tyrbwlch, Waunfach, Parcydwr, Clynmaen, Mirianog, Tybach, Llwynbedw, Pontsaeson, Gellygarn, Pontybryn, Allt y Cwmins, down to Cwmgwaun.

Friday, 13th July, 1860:
Perambulation of the Borough of Newport.
The town was decorated with flowers and triumphal arches. Horses and vehicles poured into the town from great distances by 10am. A procession was formed, headed by the band, and marched out to Llwyngwair to meet the Lloyds. The carriage containing Mrs. Lloyd and Marteine took up position at the head of the line and Mr. Lloyd on horseback fell in at the rear. They returned to Newport and to the Castle, where a jury was sworn in as follows:—
Rev. Llew. Lloyd Thomas, rector.

John Llewellyn, surgeon.
Rev. Jas. Jenkins, Baptist Minister.
Benj. Evans, Parcymarriage.
John Evans, Penfeidir.
David John, Cnwce.
Wm. Salmon, Brithdir Mawr.
David Griffiths, High Street.
Thos. Bevan, surgeon.
David Seaborn, draper.
Thos. Howells, cabinet-maker.
David Jones, currier.
David Harries, Rhigian.
Thos. Griffiths, Blaenmeini.
Richard Morris, Newport.
John Williams, chemist.

The oath was administered in English and was explained in Welsh by the Mayor, Mr. Wm. Williams, (Parke). The jury received their badge of office, a crimson rosette, from the heir, Master Marteine Lloyd. The perambulation began and included all the lands granted by Nicholas Martin to the Burgesses of Newport, and passed along Holmhouse, Starving Corner, Cerrig, Waunoerfa, Bedd Morris, Corner Llannerch, Dolrannog and down and around Carningli. Then along the Parrog and Sladefach Commons thence returning through Newport to the Castle.

In the Castle Court the horsemen formed into a circle two-deep, flanked by banners and flags. The Lord of the Barony entered the circle on horseback and addressed the company, thanking them for their attendance and also their ladies, who were present, for making the flags.

Saturday, 14th July, 1860:
The Procession left Newport at 10am for Dinas, where a Jury was sworn in. They traversed the commons of Dinas and Llanllawer, then Alltygors and Gilwer commons, thence by Tygwyn, Parcyrhos ending at Fron.

Mr. Wm. Griffith George, Steward of the Barony, Mr. John Daniel Jones, Agent of Mr. Lloyd and Mr. John Harries of Newport, are thanked for their assistance to the writer of the article.

A dinner was provided each day by Mr. Lloyd.

The last ceremonial perambulation took place in 1888.[18] It lasted five days and the procession included, in addition to the homagers and tenants, 'Pioneers in scarlet tunics with silver buttons and red caps carrying mattocks ornamented with rams' horns and rosettes' and a band on horseback. One of the Pioneers carried 'the special Boundary Flag' of blue and red surmounted with a golden eagle. Sir Marteine and Lady Lloyd were in their carriage and the procession was said to be a mile long, 'and those attending were regaled with bread and cheese and beer each day.'

In August 1964 the author revived the custom in so far as the boundaries of the borough of Newport, which coincide with those of the parish, were concerned. A number of aldermen and burgesses, together with townspeople, visitors and children, assembled on The Cross, some on horseback but most on foot, and moved off, led by the banner of the barony, in the direction of Penybont. The party went along The Marsh to the Parrog, where some boys were beaten, so that they would remember where the boundary was, and then up Feidr Brenin and past Trewreiddig to Bedd Morus, where more boys were beaten at the boundary stone, which bears the initials of Sir Thomas Davies Lloyd. Having partaken of sandwiches and ale the party moved across the open mountain to the south of Carn Ingli, and then down past Alltclydach and back to Newport. At the special court, that was held for that evening for the first time for that purpose, it was reported to the mayor that the bounds had been inspected and had been found to be in order. The custom has been held annually since that date.

Perambulation.

The Norman lords granted boroughs the right to hold fairs and markets in order to stimulate trade, and, at the same time, they benefited from the tolls that were payable on every beast that was sold and from every stall erected. Fairs were associated with the festivals of the church and were held on the feast day of the local saint, when business was combined with merry-making, as the derivation of the word 'fair' from the Latin *feriae*, 'holidays', indicates. In effect, they provided the only holidays of the year for farmers and farm-workers alike.

'The great fair', as George Owen called it, was held at Newport on the feast of St Curig.[1] His feast day is given as 16 June but when the Gregorian calendar was adopted in this country in 1752, the date was changed to 27 June. There was also a hiring fair that was held on 16 October, known as *Ffair Fach* (the Little Fair), and there are records of other fairs that were held in the town. On 13 November 1795 it was presented at the Court Leet that the fairs commonly called *Ffair Gla'mai Fach* (the little May Fair), held on 14 May, and *Ffair Fihangel Fach* (the little Michaelmas Fair), held on 10 December, should be 'tollsy fairs', that is, fairs at which tolls are levied. The list of Pembrokeshire fairs given annually in *Almanac y Cymro* in the 1880's. stated that there were fairs at Newport on '27 June. 3 August and the third Monday in October (hiring)'.[2]

The tolls were paid to the lord of Cemais and the mayor was accountable for them although, later on, he received them for his own use. They varied from 2s.6d. on the sale of a horse to 2d. for every pig sold, and there was a charge of 1d. each for 'pitchings and standings'. The net product, after deducting the cost of collection, which amounted to about one-fourth of the whole, averaged £9 a year towards the end of the last century.

The burgesses had to attend the fair with the mayor on pain of being amerced seven shillings in default. Owen Griffiths and four other burgesses were so fined for failing to attend *Ffair Gurig* in 1604.[3]

According to the toll book of the fair held on 16 June 1603,[4] the only early record extant, there were seventy-eight transactions at the fair, during which 30 head of cattle were sold, and 520 sheep and lambs. The rector, Lewis Thomas, bought a black cow from John Edward of Nevern for 29s; Harry Philip of Letterston bought a black heifer from Rice Thomas of Newport for 12s.8d., and William Melchior of Brithdir sold a black cow and a brown one to Rees ap Rees of Llandovery for £3 each. The rector sold 60 lambs at 2s. each to Robert ap Ieuan of Cardigan, and James William, weaver, Newport, got 2s.6d. each for four sheep he sold to Gruffydd ab Owen of Llanycefn. Dealers came from as far north as Llanfihangel Geneu'r Glyn, near Borth, and from Robeston West, in south Pembrokeshire. The tolls collected by the mayor, Rees Lloyd, amounted to 30s.3d. The amount of toll paid by William Melchior is not recorded and, if he did not pay, it is a matter of conjecture whether he was penalised, like Thomas William, who bought a horse at the May Fair in 1793 and, as he had not paid the accustomed toll, the Court Leet decreed that 'in accordance with our charter', the horse would become 'forfeit to the lõrd and the mayor of our corporation'.

The toll book of a fair held at Newport on 28-29 November 1825 shows that 224 cattle were sold, together with 42 horses, 43 sheep and 151 pigs, yielding tolls to the value of £10.19.10½ . Wages had to be paid out of that sum to twelve men for their services for one, two or three days, at 1s. per hour, amounting to 24s., a clerk was paid, 6s., stationery and paint cost 5s.11d., candles 2d., two quarts of ale for the 'countsmen' 8d. and ale for the watchmen 11s.6d., a total of £2.8.3, leaving a net income of £4.11.7½. The average net income from pitchings and standings was 6s, which would indicate that there were 70 to 80 stalls at each fair.

Objection to the payment of tolls grew to such an extent in the nineteenth century that horse-and-cattle dealers advertised a rival toll-free fair to be held at Maenclochog and, on 29 May 1843, the burgesses sent a petition to Thomas Lloyd, lord of Cemais, in the following terms:

> We, the burgesses of the town of Newport, having learned with deep concern that the merchants, drovers and vendors had fully and decidedly determined to move Gurig Fair, hitherto held in June in this town, to the village of Maenclochog, we greatly deplore the loss and deprivation which this town and vicinity shall sustain thereby. It has been cried in the last fair at Maenclochog that the fair will be kept there toll-free, and there are handbills widely circulated to that effect. We beg leave to enclose one in our address. Sensible of this, we most humbly yet most earnestly entreat your honour to relinquish the tolls as the only means of its preservation in this town. Should your honour condescend to comply with our request, we shall forthwith send to the weekly papers and circulate handbills that [the] fair will be continued free of tolls in this town. It comes now to this crisis: that the tolls must be remitted or the fair will become extinct. May one prevail on your honour to relinquish the tolls that the fair may be perpetuated? Will your honour condescend to accept an annual contribution of the innkeepers, shopkeepers and the inhabitants in lieu of the tolls?[6]

Thomas Lloyd had no difficulty in agreeing to the petition for, by now, the tolls went to the mayor who was allowed to benefit from the profits of the fair.[7] Even so, there was a proposal to start a rival fair at Eglwyswrw in November 1851, and an 'illegal' fair was held at Newport in October 1862.

The fair, as one remembers it before the last war, began early in the day, when the horses arrived and were lined up in West Street with their heads to the pavement on both sides of the road, so that it would be highly dangerous to walk down the middle of the road. The street was, therefore, completely blocked and any vehicle wishing to enter the town had great difficulty in passing through the array of equine haunches.

The whole length of Market Street was lined with stalls, with the overflow extending down Long Street. There would be fruit stalls with huge, juicy pears, bunches of grapes, apples, bananas, pomegranates. People would only have heard of the pomegranate in the Bible and, somehow, it seemed unreal: they took it home and peeled off its leathery orange-red skin, bit by bit to reveal the pink, transparent fruit which one ate with a pin, grain by grain. Cheapjacks shouted their heads off and

St Curig's Fair.

rattled arm-lengths of plates to the edge of breaking point to draw the attention of housewives to the unheard-of give-away bargains they were offering. There were shove-a-penny, roll-a-penny, throw-a-penny stalls and there was a coconut-stall where one could hit a coconut full in the face with a wooden ball repeatedly and it would not budge until the stall-holder felt that the shier deserved a chance and put another handful of sawdust under it when it would fall at the touch of a ball. There were shooting galleries, with airguns that seemed to have a bias that one eventually mastered sufficiently to shoot a clay pipe and win a tinsel flower, or a pink jug with a picture of Newport Castle. Drunks would sometimes shoot the jug instead of the pipe.

In the field beside Llysmeddyg, there would be a roundabout with painted horses and monster cockerels going round and round, driven by a man who stood in the middle turning a wheel, and swinging boats and, sometimes, chair-o-planes that got the girls screaming, and more stalls.

It all came to an end before the outbreak of the last war.

When the author was mayor in 1951, he revived *Ffair Gurig* to the extent of having 'pitchings and standings' in the street, set up by volunteers for local charities, and managed to persuade Mrs Peter Studt to bring her fairground equipment to the playing field. He invited the mayors of Cardigan, Haverfordwest, Tenby and Pembroke to the official opening, which turned out to be the first occasion upon which the neighbouring civic dignitaries were gathered together.

In a composition[8] made between Nicholas Martin and the freeholders of Cemais in 1278 it was agreed that the tenants were 'not to sell anything but first to offer the same to be sold at the market at Newport and there to pay toll for the same', except that after the hour of noon they were at liberty to take their goods and sell them elsewhere without having to pay toll. They could also exchange goods without paying toll, provided no money changed hands. Failure to comply with any of the conditions resulted in payment of a fine of seven shillings. Freeholders and burgesses could buy and sell anywhere without toll.

By 1603, according to George Owen, the market at Newport, and that at St David's, were 'not worth the speaking of, partly for that they be so small and bad, but especially for the abuse, for that the same is used every Sunday, before service, even about sun rising.'[9] Markets were originally held on Sundays, when everyone was free from the accustomed labour, and despite Pope Innocent III's ruling in 1200 that they should be held on a week-day, they reverted to the Sabbath. In the agreement of 1278, however, it states that the market was to be held every Thursday, and so it remained until the nineteenth century, when it was changed to Friday.[10] George Owen added that the terms of the grant of the market were no longer observed and thought its decline, 'amonge other thinges ... to have beene the chiefest causes of the decay of the towne'.

Richard Fenton noted[11] that 'about the beginning of the sixteenth century the town of Newport was very populous, and carried on an extensive woollen manufactory, but owing to a great mortality, probably from the sweating sickness, which thinned its inhabitants, and left desolation behind in this once crowded mart, it fell into decay, insomuch, that its market was discontinued; a circumstance said to have been the origin of that of Fishguard, which rose on its ruins.' Fenton also maintained that the epidemic was the cause of the destruction of Newport Bridge because it was believed that the inhabitants of the Morfa district had carried the disease into the town.

No direct evidence of such a sickness has been traced but the prevalence of a disease in the following century may be gathered from an order of the Quarter Sessions of the county of Pembroke,[12] when Haverfordwest was ravaged by the bubonic plague in 1652, that the high constables of Cemais should, 'touching the relief of Newport', make payment of 'one moiety of the rate for [the relief of] Haverfordwest to the town of Newport' and 'that the justices of the peace take special care not only for the said towns but for other places where the sickness is and if necessary meet every fortnight for the purpose.'

The rental of 1594 maintained that a revival of the market 'wold cause the towne to florish againe',[13] but there is no evidence of a conscious effort to do so until the early part of the eighteenth century when, at the Court Leet held on 25 September 1713, 'the Grand Jury presented a market to be necessary in the town on Thursday weekly, according as it was formerly and ought to be kept as usually.' Counsel's opinion[14] revealed that the market, in or before a 'sickness of 1665 was for the better convenience of the inhabitants and country adjacent to the borough of Newport moved into a village about four miles distant from the said borough and by the voluntary meeting of the people the said market has been ever since the said sickness kept and upheld at the said village.' The lord of Cemais entered into an agreement with the Court Leet for 'the renewal of the Thursday market'.

That the market prospered following its revival is indicated by the presentment at the Court Leet held on 16 April 1800 that the Mayor 'attend the market every Friday to look over the weights and measures, or put one in his stead', and by the holding of a public meeting at the Llwyngwair Arms at 11 a.m. on 19 November 1858 'for the purpose of taking into consideration the propriety and advantage of building a Market House' at Newport. There is no evidence that it was decided to proceed with the building.

The market continued to function until the 1930's. Horse-drawn carts, covered with pig-nets, brought in litters of porkers and, having unhitched the horses, waited in line at the top of Market Street for buyers, and farmers and their wives came heavily laden with large baskets full of fresh eggs and farm butter.

After the market disappeared, the public houses still remained open all day on Fridays, and when an attempt was made by the police to withdraw the extension of permitted hours, the magistrates listened to the plea that country people continued to come to town on Fridays to do their shopping and required refreshment.

There were twenty-four public houses in Newport at the beginning of this century, 'apart from gin-shops and shebeens', but some of them were closed soon after, as a result of the Evan Roberts revival of 1904. The editor of the *County Echo* was proud to report, in February of the following year, that 'as her practical contribution to the great revival movement, Miss [Blanche] Evans of the Plough Inn, Newport, did not apply at the local Petty Sessions for the renewal of the licence', which he regarded as 'an unprecedented example of Christian devotion and the severest test of true earnestness'. Other hostelries surrendered their licences under the weight of higher taxes on the licensed trade, or took advantage of the compensation that was being offered for closure.

One of the earliest extant references to a local inn is contained in a lease for two lives granted by George Bowen of Llwyngwair in 1790 to John Hughes, yeoman, of 'the Green Dragon in East Street, Park y llan, Park yr exciseman, and Knwc y Watch, near the east end of the town of Newport'. His grandson, George Bowen, on 9 October 1830, gave William Owen, victualler, 'a lease for three lives of a house called *The Golden Lion*, formerly known as *The Green Dragon*'[15]. The new name could have reference to the golden lion in the Bowen coat-of-arms. Cnwc-y-watch was an alternate name for Spite, or *Tavern Spite*, at the corner of New Road and the road to Pen-y-bont.

Llys Meddyg stands on the site of the *Masons' Arms*, which later became known as the *Prince of Wales Inn*, when it served as a coaching inn from which Mr Jackson's *Shah*, and other coaches, left for Crymych railway station.

At the lower end of Upper St Mary Street was the *Globe Inn*, which remained open until about 1930, and next door was the *Rose and Crown*, which closed before the Great War when the house was renamed Teifi House.

The Justices' Room was built on the site of the *Britannia Inn*, next door, to the *Llwyngwair Arms* where the Court Baron and Court Leet have met since the latter part of the last century. The *Angel Hotel* became the *Angel Temperance Hotel* and is now Angel House, in Long Street.

In Market Street there was *London House,* later Fountain House, the *Jolly Tar* now a garage between Bon Marché and the *Barley Mow,* which remained open until the late 1920's. At the top of the street, where Gwynfi House stands, was the *Ship,* formerly the *Ship and Castle* where a meeting of bards was held on Whit-Monday, 23 May 1774, at which Ioan Siencyn was present. In Church Steet, the *Pig and Whistle* stood where Coedfryn is now. The *Rising Sun* is now 'Carningli', on the road to Cilgwyn, and near Felin Cilgwyn, was the *Bridgend Inn.*

The *Castle Inn* has '(Commercial)' added after its name in Pigot's Directory of 1830. Before the end of the century it had become the *Commercial Hotel* and it remained so until the 1970's when it was renamed the *Castle Hotel.*

Royal Oak, the second most popular inn sign in the country derives from the escape of Charles II by hiding in an oak tree at Boscobel after the battle of Worcester in 1651. Air Commodore James Bevan Bowen told the author that he was of the opinion that the inn at Newport was so named because a Captain Hugh Bowen of Llwyngwair, who for his services, was in line to receive a knighthood in the Order of the Royal Oak which the king had planned to establish to commemorate his ambuscade.

The west end of the town was not well served as it had only the *Plough Inn,* now Welford House, and the *Farmers' Arms,* now Porthmeor.

There were four public houses on the Parrog: the *Queen's,* or *Queen's Head* (Morfan), the *Sloop Inn* (Beach View and Kosy Kot), the *Parrog Arms* (Morawelon), and the *Ship Afloat* (Seagull Cottage), together with the *Mariners' Arms,* beyond Bettws, which surrendered its licence in January 1903.

The Commercial (now Castle) Hotel 1904.

THE PORT OF NEWPORT

Despite having a 'barred haven to serve a small ship with a westerly or northerly wind upon a string', as Thomas Phaer put it in his *Report on the Harbours and Customs Administration of Wales under Edward VI* (1547-53), the estuary of the river Nevern has provided harbourage for those who sailed the seas from earliest times. There are traces of its use by prehistoric people, and by seafaring saints, and it is probable that the Norman invader cast anchor in the bay, and certain that his successors made use of it to maintain contact with their kin in the west of England.

In addition to being disadvantaged by being 'a barred haven' on account of a sandbank across its estuary, the port facilities were also dependent upon the tide, the range of which is just over fourteen feet.[1] This maximum difference between high and low water takes place at spring tides, which occur when the moon is new and when it is full. In approximate terms, the tide rises one twelfth of its total height during the first hour of its flow, two-twelfths during the second hour, three-twelfths each during the third and fourth, two-twelfths during the fifth, and a twelfth in the sixth, and it ebbs in the same proportionality. The high tides peak at around nine o'clock (GMT) night and morning, and the neap tides, correspondingly, are at their lowest at about three o'clock (GMT) at night and in the afternoon. Persistent south-westerlies in St George's Channel have a tendency to cause the tides to be earlier and higher than predicted, and north-easterly winds are inclined to have the reverse effect.

The tide coming in.

Evidence of the emergence of Newport as a trading port dates from the sixteenth century. George Owen, who, as Deputy Vice-Admiral of South Wales was primarily interested in the defences of the Pembrokeshire coast, complained that the recruitment of rank and file for that purpose had been made more difficult because the county, 'especially of late years is fallen much to trade to sea, and a great part of the county's people are seamen and mariners'.[2]

In order to establish effective control over the coasting trade, and in an effort to suppress piracy along the Welsh coast, a survey[3] was made of 'all crekes havons and landing places'. These were grouped under the head-ports of Cardiff, Chester and Milford Haven, to which Customs officials were posted in 1559. Commissioners were appointed to undertake the survey and, of the four selected for the county of Pembroke, Arnold Butler of Coedcenlas had died before he received the commission, and John Bradshaw of St Dogmael's was found to be resident in Radnorshire, leaving Thomas Catharne of Prendergast and John Rastall, justice of Great Sessions, to undertake the survey. They made a list of thirty-two 'portes crekes havens and landing places' around the Pembrokeshire coast only five of which were along the north coast: Porthmawr (Whitesand Bay), Trefin, Fishguard, Newport and St Dogmael's. They appointed deputies to carry out the work, and divided the coast into ten stretches for that purpose. For the stretch between Fishguard and Cardigan Bridge they appointed Morgan ab Owen, Thomas Williams, David Thomas and Philip Philpyn.[4]

Measures were taken to reorganise the administration of the Customs Revenue for which special 'parchment books' were supplied by the Exchequer to the local Customs officials.[5] These 'Welsh Port Books' show that between 1565 and 1603, the number of Pembrokeshire-owned vessels varied between eighteen and twenty-six, most of which were less than twenty tons.

The only ship recorded as trading out of Newport was the *Saviour* (6 tons) belonging to Owen Picton which, with a crew of three, 'useth comonly to trade to Ireland, North Wales and upp Severne afishinge'.[6] It sailed for Bristol on 18 July 1566, when it was described in the Port Book as *Le Saviour de Newbergo in Kemes,* with John Roberts as master, carrying '1 pack and fardel [bundle] of friezes [coarse woollen cloth with a nap on one side] and 11,000 slate stones'.

Cloth, and wool, were the principal coastwise exports of the county in the sixteenth century, forming up to two-thirds of the outgoing shipments, but by 1585 the export of cloth had dwindled, and it continued to do so, largely on account of the competition in the English markets of better cloth produced elsewhere.[7] The export of wool increased, however, as the cloth industry declined and, as George Owen observed, 'the county abounded with sheep as never before'.[8] In south Pembrokeshire, he stated, merchants from the West Country came twice a year to buy the wool, but in Cemais it was 'bought by north Wales men and wrought by them into white cloth which they sell to Shrewsbury men'. He regretted that the trade of clothing had been neglected. especially as there was twice as much wool shorn as there was forty years previously, when it was 'all wrought within the shire and sold in friezes'.[9]

The woollen factory in Upper Bridge Street, and the one that formerly stood in Mill Lane, were powered by Afon y Felin, which had already driven the millstones of the Castle Mill. James Jones, of the Mill Lane factory, who was a leading figure at Ebenezer Congregational Chapel,[10] died in 1902, and his brother, Samuel Jones of Gweunydd, who is described as a weaver, was also prominent in the chapel's affairs until his death, at the age of eighty, in 1880. Vaughan Francis continued to manufacture Welsh flannel at the Upper Bridge Street factory up to the Great War.

Typical of cottage factories was the house facing the Memorial Hall where Daniel Lewis y Gwehydd (the weaver) sat at his spinning wheel on the ground floor and, when he had spun enough wool, went upstairs to weave it on his pedal-driven loom.

Lewis Morris, in the notes to his plan of Newport harbour in 1748," stated that 'corn and butter are here in plenty, as also herrings and other fish. In this bay is a quarry of slates, which supplies all this coast; and not far from there is a vein of alum earth, never worked.'

Slate-quarrying was carried on in the Ordovician shale slab cliffs of the bays that lie west of Y Cwm: Traeth Samwel, Chwarel Ffeiradon (the Priests' Quarry), Aber Step and Brodan in which, at low water, are displayed the best examples of wave-cut platforms in Pembrokeshire. George Owen referred to the quality of the 'black slate' found in these sea-cliffs, which produced tiles that were 'so fine of colour, plain and smooth, they will serve to write with any bodkin or to draw any picture of beast, fowl and such like very fair, as also to make dials, and will be very easily carved or graven. These stones are very large and thin, nothing inferior for colour, thinness and enduring to those set from beyond the seas which are laid on the Royal Exchange as also on divers turrets and new buildings in the city of London.'[12] He adds that they are 'sent by water to Haverford, Pembroke and Tenby and to divers parts of Ireland and sold by the thousand.'

The quarries were still being worked in the middle of the last century, for Samuel Lewis[13] in 1848 recorded that 'the trade principally carried on' at Newport was 'the working of some extensive quarries of slate, with which the neighbouring coast abounds, and of which great quantities are shipped to various places, the vessels being enabled to approach close to the quarries and to receive the slates from the overhanging cliffs: and in the burning of lime for the supply of the adjacent districts, in which a considerable portion of the population is employed.' He, too, stated that 'a vein of alum shale is said to lie within a short distance of the town, but it has never been worked'

George Owen stated that tuff stone, a rock formed by consolidation of volcanic ashes, was 'found on the mountain over Newport' which being 'a large stone very tough yet easy in hewing' was made into mantel pieces, door frames, coign-stones, 'but above all things it served best for stairs whereon a man may boldly tread without sliding'.[14]

'Another great blessing,' he wrote, was the abundance of herrings which were taken all along the coast as if the county was 'enclosed with a hedge of herrings'.[15] The rental roll of 1594 reported that herring fishing yielded 'greate commoditie to the inhabitantes of the towne and countreye thereabowtes'. Herrings gather in vast shoals twice each year, in the spring and in the autumn, for the purpose of spawning. The spring spawn takes place near the coast and, in the case of Pembrokeshire, in the upper reaches of Milford Haven. In autumn they spawn in deeper water and the fishermen of Newport, from September onward, would harvest the fish with long, fine-meshed drift nets that were held in an upright position by cork floats and lead weights, and set far out in the bay. Each member of the boat crew would provide a length of fishing net, and failure to do so was punishable. At the Court Baron held on 5 August 1611, Owen John complained that James Lewis had failed to fulfil a promise made the previous November to 'supply five nets for herring fishing and to place them in the boat of Rees Lloyd, gent.' in which they were to fish together.

The herrings were sold by the meise,[16] a measure of five 'hundred' fish, the 'hundred' being 120. The herrings were counted in forties, with a 'warp' of one fish being thrown to one side for each forty to keep tally, and another, known as a 'tale' to mark each 'hundred', so that a meise comprised 620 herrings. The catch was shared equally among the crew, with an extra share for the owner of the boat.

In Elizabethan times herrings from Newport and Fishguard went to feed the Queen's armies in Spain and in the 1740's a thousand barrels of cured herrings were being exported each year to Bristol, Wexford, Dublin and to the Mediterranean countries. By 1800 the trade had begun to decline and, in 1848, Samuel Lewis reported that 'a herring-fishery exists here but the demand is so inconsiderable that it is not productive of much benefit to the persons engaged in it'.[17] Fishing for herring, nonetheless, continued up to the early part of the twentieth century.

The burgesses had common of piscary,[18] that is, the right to take fish, in the river Nevern from its mouth to its confluence with the river Clydach, which is the highest point to which ordinary tides flow, 'by speciall graunt from the lord, whereby,' the 1594 extent states, 'the saide burgesses have oftentymes greate store of fishe taken as salmons, suins and other fishe.' One half of 'one weir on the water of Nevarne with the free fishery there' was valued at 13s.4d. yearly.

Fishing for salmon and sewin, or sea trout, at the estuary of the river Nevern was carried out, as on other estuarine waters throughout Britain, by seine netting. The seine net, so named from the Latin *sagena*, 'a drag net', is up to 350 yards in length and from ten to twelve feet deep, according to the depth of the water to be fished, with cork floats and lead weights to keep it upright in the water.

The net was laid in the body of the nineteen-foot black-tarred rowing boat built for the purpose by David Williams of Aberystwyth, which normally had a crew of five men beside the owner of the boat, who was the captain. Before the last war, there were two such boats at Y Cwm, one belonging to Evan 'Ianto' Davies, who had three sons in his crew, and the other to John Selby, who had two. Each took its turn to fish the *ergyd*, or station, allotted to it along the edge of the sea on Traeth Mawr. The most prized *ergyd* was the one nearest the estuary and was known as Y Llygad (the Eye), or Gene'r Afon (the mouth of the river); next to it was Y Dor (the belly), and next to that Y Tynn Segur (the idle pull). The team

The Nevern estuary from Cwm.

that fished *Y Llygad* today, had *Y Dor* tomorrow, and *Y Tynn Segur* the day after. Two other stations could be fished on an incoming tide: *Y Bened*, opposite The Bennett, and *Pen Ucha'r Tra'th* (the top end of the beach). The team fishing *Y Llygad* could go on to *Y Bened* on the flood,

High tide at Parrog.

65

and that fishing *Y Dor* to *Pen Ucha'r Tra'th,* which was considered the best station after *Y Llygad.* Fishing was not allowed on Saturday and Sunday, when the crews would often sit on the rock above Cwm watching salmon leap in the bay before entering the estuary.

A boat could not set out until *Y Garreg Fach,* also called *Ynys Patmos,* showed its 'whiskers' above the ebbing tide. With the captain steering, two of the men would row the boat out over the bar and make for the shore to drop a shoreman holding a rope with one end of the net. The other two paid out the net over the side of the boat in a half-moon until the other end was brought ashore. Having made fast the boat, the men, three at each end, steadily hauled the net in. When they came to the central section of the net, known as *y rhwyd got* (the short net), which was made of stronger stuff as it held the 'catch', the bottom was hauled in faster than the top so as to prevent any fish escaping. The salmon and the sewin were swiftly dispatched with a small truncheon, called 'the priest'.

The seine fishers wore old clothes with a rope tied round the waist. The end of the rope was hitched to the net rope so as to transfer the strain to the whole body and make the pulling easier. This rope was likened to a monkish girdle and used to add credence to the legendary belief that the method of fishing was so-called because it was practised on the Seine and that it had been brought to the vicinity by the monks who had been imported to found St Dogmael's Abbey in the twelfth century.[19]

Seine netting was allowed on the river between Newport Bridge and 'an imaginary line drawn across the said river from Dinas Head to Pen-y-bâl at the estuary of Nevern', as laid down in the bye-laws of the South-West Wales Fishery Board. When inclement weather prevented boats going to sea, it was permitted to use a wade net to fish the river, except that the crew due to fish *Y Llygad* was not allowed to draw the river that day.

Coracles were used on the Nevern up to the latter part of the last century[20]. The evidence laid before the 'Commissioners Appointed to inquire into the Salmon Fisheries' in 1861 revealed that 'no more than four coracles based on Newport operated above the tideway'. The Commissioners found that the coraclemen were in conflict with 'the men that fish the sand' and concluded that the coraclemen 'who fish the river' were 'the men who gave the most trouble', and that the seine-fishermen 'at the mouth of the river are fair fishermen'. It is likely that David Thomas and Thomas Hughes, who were amerced at the Court Leet held on 12 October 1612 for taking 'small salmon in the river Nevern near the bridge of the town' were coraclemen.[21]

Among the trades of the town, at one time, was tanning.[22] In 1529 John Lloyd of Hendre, St. Dogmael's, granted to 'one John of Newport a lease of a burgage, garden and four acres bounde by the lands of John Butler, Sir James ab Owen, Thomas Perrot, called Rigyan; Great Lacke, a brook called Clayne Hyrre [Llain Hir], and a place called The Lyttyl Tanhouse.' A report[23] of about this time stated that hides were being sold at exorbitantly high prices at Newport, and at Tenby, before the culprits were brought to justice.

A malthouse stood at the junction of Parrog Road and Feidr Ganol, until it became the depot of the Cardigan and District Agricultural Co-operative Society, selling coal and culm and corn and agricultural implements.

The main imports were coal, culm and limestone, and commodites that the community did not itself produce, which were mainly items of domestic use or requirements for the promotion of local industry.[24] On 16 August 1566, the *Saviour de Newporte* brought from Bristol a cargo comprising '1 ton 1 hogshead iron, 2 hogshead train oil, 1 barrel tar, 2 and a half ton pitch, half cwt hops, half cwt alum, 1 quarter white soap, 1 bolt Poldavi, 1 chest dry wares, 1 fardel linen, 14 bows, 1 barrel teasels, 3 barrels salt'. A similar cargo[25] from Bristol, arrived on 12 September, except that it also contained '1 ballet *crassum* . . . half cwt black soap, 2 doz. hand cards'. Alum and teasels were employed in the woollen industry; iron, train oil, tar and pitch were required for ship-building, and so was Poldavi, a rough canvas used as sail-cloth and named after Poldavid, near Douarnenez, where it was woven, and the ballet, or small ball, of crassum, a coarse thread for stitching the sail-cloth. Salt was needed for salting pigs and herrings. In 1876 the *Spread Eagle* (26 tons) brought a cargo of salt from Gloucester, which appears to have been a regular source of supply.

Thomas Phaer, in his *Anglia Wallia* (c 1552),[26] maintained that the Newport area was 'bare of corn but plenty enough of cattle', and stated that grain was regularly imported. In 1883 the *Kelly* (24 tons) brought a cargo of barley from Milford, and at least one shipload arrived each year for the following ten years.

Other imports included bricks and ware from Chester, in the *Favourite* (32 tons) in 1876, and bricks and tiles came from Bridgwater in the *George Evans* in 1877, while ship-loads of bricks alone arrived fairly regularly from Cardigan. Manure and superphosphate, and one consignment of guano, were imported, mainly from Milford, and there were cargoes of freestone and 'stones' from there. Vessels carrying merchandise, invariably from Bristol, would call at various ports offering their wares. A poster dated 27 July 1838 announced that 'new *Packet of Cardigan* (a constant trader), Thomas Evans, master', was loading at the Cardigan pier, Welsh Back, Bristol, for 'Cardigan, Newcastle (Emlyn), Cenarth, Newport, Boncath, Pontresely, Eglwyswrw and places adjacent'. The master sometimes took his wife to sea with him to assist him in the purchase, and sale, of the goods. Owen Evans, the master of the *Martha,* claimed to be the last ship that was built on Parrog Bach, took his wife, Nancy, as cook and depended upon her to help him select the crockery and fine china that he carried and sold as a sideline.[27]

Limestone, coal and culm far exceeded all other imports. Coal was required for domestic use, and so was culm, which was anthracite coal dust, five parts of which, and one of clay, were mixed with water, so that the mixture looked like black mortar. It was taken by the handful and tossed into oval 'balls', the size of a goose egg, and laid on the fire. At night, after raking out the ash, which was pinkish in colour, a shovelful of culm was placed on the fire so that it would last until the morning. A culm fire was never allowed to burn itself out, as this was considered unlucky and, if it

Limekiln at Parrog.

should do so, it could only be rekindled by 'borrowing' fire from a neighbour. Culm was also necessary for burning lime.

Slaked lime was used for lime-washing the walls of cottages and houses, both within and without, but it was put to far greater use to counter the acidity of the soil in north Pembrokeshire by spreading it on the land. George Owen observed, in 1603,[28] that 'liming has been more used within these thirty or forty years than in times past, and it destroys the furze, fern, heath and other like shrubs growing on the land, and brings forth a fine and sweet grass and quite changes the hue and face of the ground, and has greatly enriched those that use it.' The limestone, after being hewn as stones of the size of a man's fist, so that it would burn the sooner, was placed in a kiln over a culm fire. After burning, and cooling, it was drawn through the 'eye' of the kiln and loaded on to a cart and taken on to the land, where it was left in heaps to await the next rain to slake it ready for spreading. 'The ground being thus amended', stated Owen, 'bears great abundance of corn for six or seven years and then requires some rest, but it is better for ever after the liming.'

The limestone was quarried, notably in the West Williamston Quarries, which could be approached along cut channels by barges of up to twenty tons that transferred their cargoes to coastal vessels at Lawrenny. The culm was also brought from the south of the county, and in particular from the Hook Colliery.

At low tide, limestone was discharged as soon as the vessel dropped anchor by throwing the stones overboard into the water, and it would then be carted to the limekilns after the tide had

Horses and carts wait to unload a schooner.

receded. Otherwise, like coal and culm, it was raised from the ship's hold in large baskets that were hauled up by a winch but, before that, by a horse that was led up and down the beach, pulling a rope over a system of pulleys. The baskets were emptied into a waiting horse-drawn cart. The carters worked until it was dark, and before daybreak, so that the vessel could discharge its cargo in time to sail out on the next tide.

According to Walter Davies (Gwallter Mechain) who carried out a survey of agriculture in south Wales in 1814,[29] permanent limekilns were erected during the second half of the eighteenth century, when they were built in almost every bay and creek along the north Pembrokeshire coast, and in the south also along the Carboniferous Limestone exposures. Newport had the largest concentration on the north coast, with one at Aber Forest, one near Bryncyn (SN 063397), one near New Mill, and four on the Parrog. One of these was built in 1777, with the consent of the Court Leet, by Thomas Mathias, and in 1788 the Court gave permission for John Lloyd, Jnr., to build 'a small storehouse for use of limeburners to sleep'. A Court Roll of 1751[30] granted permission for two limekilns to be built, one by James Bowen of Llwyngwair and Thomas Knolles of Wenallt, and the other by Owen Lewis, 'in Bridge Street', that is, at Penybont, and for another to be built at the lower end of St Mary Street by William Warren of Trewern. All three were erected on the manorial waste, probably on The Marsh, and consent was furthermore given for a limekiln to be erected 'in the High Street', that is, Market Street. There is no trace of any of these, and two of the limekilns on the Parrog were wantonly destroyed in the second half of the twentieth century. A fine double-kiln survives and, beside it, a cottage that was occupied by a limeburner. The kilns were kept burning day and night and had to be fed and raked regularly, so that the limeburner's task was unceasing and dangerous.

The course of the river changed from time to time which rendered the entrance to the harbour even more hazardous. Lewis Morris, in 1748, warned that the bar across the river 'is now very dangerous by the River's being drove to the Rocks on the South side; there are old Piles to be seen at low water Mark where the Bar hath formerly been, and where it still ought to be', and he came to the conclusion that a 'rolling of Porcupines [i.e. rollers with projecting spikes] over the Sand, to bring the River into its original Channel, is the only Improvement that can be made here at present.'[31].

To meet the needs of trading, at least five storehouses were built on the Parrog. In 1758, the Court Leet presented that John Lloyd be granted consent to enclose land, on payment of chief rent, for the purpose of erecting a store house of four couples, and, in the following year John James had 'liberty to build a store house on the Parrog'. In 1787 John Hughes was given the same facility to erect another. In 1792, William Lloyd was given permission to extend his storehouse by fourteen feet and, in the following year, Essex Bowen, a younger son of James Bowen of Llwyngwair who had served as a Captain in the Royal Marines, was permitted to enclose a yard along side his storehouse.

The storehouses were built to receive and store the merchandise carried by the little ships. Only one now remains, and its future has been secured through its acquisition and adaptation as the Newport Boat Club. The remains of two others are traceable. One was demolished in 1922, following a wager between its owner and the reigning mayor, who won

Newport Boat Club, formerly a storehouse built c 1825.

and was able to transport its stone for use in building the Memorial Hall.

The dry-stone quay walls were built of slates, set on edge, that were brought from the sea-quarries in the cliffs beyond Pen Catman. The Quay Wall was built in 1816 and, on 30 June 1824, the Court Leet presented that John Davies, merchant, be allowed to build a quay at Parrog 'between his present storehouse and the sea' and, in April of the following year, Captain Daniel Evans and John Jenkins were given permission to build 'a quay from Captain Evans's New Quay unto John Jenkins's Quay.'[32]

Newport became known for its shipbuilding in the eighteenth century and an early account of a launching was provided by the local poet, John Jenkins (Ioan Siencyn), who was born in 1716 the son of Siencyn Thomas, a cobbler-poet of Cwm Du, Llechryd. He was appointed school master at Nevern, under the Circulating Schools scheme of Griffith Jones, Llanddowror, in 1754, and he remained there until he was within three years of his death, in 1796. For a period of six years he was given accommodation at Cwmgloyn, where he taught the poor to read under the patronage of the squire, Thomas Lloyd.

Thomas Lloyd, a Justice of the Peace and High Sheriff of Pembrokeshire in 1771, a bachelor and the last of the Lloyds of Cwmgloyn, was described as 'an improving landlord'. He owned three ships, two of which inspired Ioan Siencyn: the *Greyhound* (70 tons)[33] built at Aberystwyth but trading from Newport, and the schooner *Hawk* (50 tons)[34] at its launching at Newport. He wished the schooner *bon voyage* as it left 'blossoming Trefdraeth for the foaming, abounding sea, and prophesied that Neptune and Triton would protect it, that it would convey the Squire to dine with his friends where he would hear tell of his

Boats at anchor.

71

ancestors, and listen to *cywydd* and *englyn* and the odes of Taliesin, as he drank his fill of the golden barley beer. Saunders Lewis chose this poem as 'a peg' for a broadcast talk he gave on the Welsh poetic tradition, in which he asked the listener to imagine:

that a poet of the fifteenth century, some great figure such as Tudur Aled, had been released to revisit Pembrokeshire at the launching of the *Hawk*, and had listened to the reading of Ioan Siencyn's verses to squire Lloyd. What would our fifteenth century master have thought or said? He would note with warm approval the occasion of the poem . . . and . . . would have relished Ioan Siencyn's development of the image of the *Hawk* as it was launched on the water:

Spread now your wings, forget the green wodlands
Learn to live 'mid the mouthing of seas.

. . . And as the poem grew to the final eulogy of squire Lloyd and his society, to the reference to Taliesin and talk of the deeds of his forefathers storied over the yellow beer on the laden dining table, Tudur Aled might well explain: "My art still survives in this last decade of the eighteenth century and the great technique and the old mastery are not all forgotten. This country poet, this Ioan Siencyn, is truly an heir of our ancient discipline . . . and I recognise him as a poet of the long line that began with Taliesin in the North." There, I think, we capture something essential in the progress of Welsh poesy. We call it the literary tradition of Wales. It means you cannot pluck a flower of song off a headland in Dyved in the late eighteenth century without stirring a great Northern star of the sixth century.[35]

The *Hawk*, which was sunk by the French, was one of less than a dozen ships built at Newport during the second half of the eighteenth century, but the rate of ship-building increased rapidly in the early part of the following century.

Most of these ships were built by John Havard, a burgess whose death was presented at the Court Leet held on 25 October 1839, and who was buried two days later at St. Mary's churchyard, where his tombstone records that he was a 'ship-builder' and that he was 69 years of age at his death.[36] His son, Levi Havard, of Dandre, followed him in the trade. He was born in 1812 and was mayor of the town in 1850-51. He died on 28 October 1881 and is buried also in the churchyard.

There were no shipyards, as such, at Newport and the vessels were usually built on a level piece of ground, preferably close to the water. The ships, whenever possible, were built of oak grown in the local woods: the planks of which the *Hawk* was built had been grown in Cwmhebog, on land belonging to Thomas Lloyd. A sawpit, such as the one on Parrog Bach, was employed to saw the heavy timber, using a long saw worked by two men, the top-sawyer on a platform above, and the bottom-sawyer in the pit. The iron fittings, including the anchors, were made by a blacksmith in his smithy, such as the one that John Davies was allowed, by the Court Leet to build on common land on the Parrog in 1835. On average, it took six months to build a vessel. As well as on the Parrog, ships were built in the small creek near Bryncyn.

The type of vesssel[37] most commonly built at Newport in the latter part of the eighteenth and nineteenth centuries was the sloop, a single-masted ship, fore and aft rigged, with mainsail and gaff topsail. Next came the brig, two-masted and square-rigged, and designed for deep sea sailing, and also the snow, a modified version of the brig. The tombstone of David Gilbert (1745-1821)[38] in St. Mary's churchyard describes him as the master of the brig *Ceturah* of Newport, 'the first brig built at the port'. From the 1820's the schooner was the type of vessel predominantly built, fore and aft rigged with two, three or even four, masts, which was easier to handle and required a smaller crew. The sloop-rigged vessel known as a flat, which was characteristic of north Wales, was represented at Newport by the *Oak* (33 tons) built at Queensferry in 1840,[39] and the *Price Jones* (23 tons) built at Flint in 1859 and owned by David Jenkins, master mariner of Newport in 1861.The latter was acquired by Thomas Roach and continued in service up to the 1914-18 war.

Among the ships that were built at Newport between 1760 and 1850,[40] most of them by John and Levi Havard (marked H), were:

	1762	*Ann & Mary*, sloop 22 tons.
H	1773	*Rose*, sloop 27 tons.
H	1777	*Betty*, sloop 24 tons.
	1789	*Charming Peggy*, sloop 63 tons.
H	1790	*William & Anne*, sloop 88 tons.
H	1792	*Elizabeth & Mary*, sloop 60 tons.
H	1795	*Flora*, sloop 28 tons.
	1800	*Ardent*, snow 120 tons.
H	1801	*Fanny Anne*, sloop 22 tons.
H	1802	*Jupiter*, sloop 64 tons.
H	1804	*Charlotte*, schooner 74 tons.
H	1804	*Culloden*, brig 83 tons.
H	1805	*Hope*, sloop 21 tons.
H	1810	*Mary Anne*, sloop 28 tons.
H	1811	*Victory*, brig 118 tons.
	1812	*Hope*, sloop 42 tons.
H	1812	*Valiant*, brig 144 tons.
H	1813	*David*, sloop 35 tons.
H	1814	*Artuose* brig 150 tons.
H	1814	*Diligence*, brig 114 tons.
H	1814	*Elice*, brig 145 tons.
H	1815	*Venerable*, brig 130 tons.
H	1816	*Ant*, brig 136 tons.
H	1817	*Ardent*, snow 125 tons.
	1817	*Friendship*, brig 83 tons.
H	1819	*Mary*, sloop 53 tons.
H	1821	*Minerva*, brig 102 tons.
	1822	*Eliza*, sloop 16 tons.
H	1823	*Hope*, brig 150 tons.
	1824	*Charlotte*, schooner 81 tons.
	1824	*Mary & Eliza*, sloop 129 tons.
H	1825	*Lady Day*, schooner 128 tons.
H	1825	*Swift*, sloop 39 tons.

H 1826 *Elizabeth,* schooner 128 tons.
H 1826 *Hope,* brig 112 tons.
H 1826 *Providence,* sloop 28 tons.
H 1827 *Hope,* snow 182 tons.
H 1827 *Betsy,* sloop 24 tons.
H 1828 *Brothers* schooner 99 tons.
H 1828 *Grace,* schooner 103 tons.
H 1829 *Harmony,* schooner 95 tons.
　 1830 *David,* schooner 26 tons.
H 1831 *Reform,* sloop 14 tons.
H 1832 *Ocean,* brig 120 tons.
H 1832 *William & Anne,* schooner 88 tons.
H 1834 *Agenoria,* brigantine 117 tons.
H 1835 *Alert,* sloop 33 tons.
H 1835 *Claudia,* schooner 103 tons.
H 1837 *Adroit,* schooner 72 tons.
　 1837 *Anne & Betsy,* smack 22 tons.
H 1837 *Jane,* schooner 78 tons.
H 1839 *Elizabeth,* sloop 27 tons.
H 1839 *Phoebe,* schooner 123 tons.
H 1842 *Ann,* brig 161 tons.

The shipping trade in Cardigan and Newport during the first half of the nineteenth century was dominated by the Davies family who, between them, owned over fifty ships, the quays on both banks of the Teifi, and storehouses and other property at Newport.[41] They established the Cardigan Mercantile Company, and founded a merchant bank at Cardigan. Thomas, the elder brother, lived at Bridge House, Cardigan, next to the Grosvenor Hotel, and his son, David, bought Castle Green. His brother, Captain John Davies, married Ann Evan of Newport and settled there, and had six sons and two daughter. Llywelyn, the eldest son, took to the sea at an early age, and married Mary, daughter of Captain Owen Harries of Newport in 1814. After several commands, he became master of the *Albion*[42] in which he took a party of eighty emigrants from north Wales to Canada. The voyage is commemorated in a prose narrative entitled *Hanes Mor-daith y Brig Albion, Aberteifi, (Llywelyn Davies, Llywydd) gyda mudolion (emigrants) &c. o Gaer-narfon i Ogledd America . . . wedi ei 'sgrifennu yn ddyddiol gan y Llywydd (Captain), &c.* (An account of the Voyage of the brig *Albion* of Cardigan, Llywelyn Davies, Captain, with emigrants from Caernarfon to North America . . . written daily by the Captain &c.). The diarist, however, signs himself *Cyfaill* (Friend), and he gives a detailed account of an emigrant voyage, in which the master is portrayed in flattering terms.

The ship left Caernarfon, with eighty emigrants aboard, on 21 May 1818 and, at one o'clock in the following afternoon, it dropped anchor in Newport Bay 'off Pistyll Brynach', and a description of the view from the ship is given:

We saw the white houses of the town, some scattered among the trees, the church tower tall and white; the two lofty towers of the ruined castle: a pleasant sight, the earth looking green and promising. To the south, above the town, a fairly high mountain rose to a rocky summit, bare except for heather. To the north-east, a high, steep rock and beyond it, good land facing south; here and there a man sowing seed. All looking as if the smile of providence were upon the land.

The master went ashore to see his wife and small daughter, and some of the passengers went off to do some shopping. They got what they wanted and 'were shown much kindness and attention', but the beer was 'very poor stuff', and so they did not take any with them. The townspeople came to gaze at them, 'a load of Welsh people about to leave their country and to face a long voyage.' Some wanted to join them, but the master refused to take them. He became aware, however, that there was a demand for emigrant berths, which the Davies family set out to provide during the next two decades.

The following morning, 'some gentlemen' came aboard to inspect the emigrants' quarters. Llywelyn returned at eleven o'clock, accompanied by his father, Captain John Davies, and the wives of some of the crewmen, who came to wish them a safe voyage, and the ship set sail at noon. It arrived at Perth Amboy, New Jersey, forty-five days later, on 7 July, after a good crossing. Llywelyn then sold his ballast of slates, which he always took, either from Cilgerran or from the cliff quarries at Newport, and sailed for home with a cargo of timber.

The *Albion* was a square-sterned snow, a modified brig, of 166 tons burthen, built in 1815 by William Roberts of Hakin, who was to marry Llywelyn's sister, Margaret, seven years later. It was owned by a syndicate comprising members of the Davies family, together with Captain Owen Harries, Llywelyn's father-in-law, and Captain Daniel Evans of Newport, all master mariners, and John Owen, farmer, of Rhosmaen, Nevern. Farmers frequently held a share in a ship that was primarily used for carrying limestone, culm or coal. Ownership, by tradition, was divided into sixty-four shares and the minimum holding, of four shares, was known as 'an ounce'.

The *Albion* foundered on the notorious Arklow Banks in 1819, and all hands were lost.

Thomas and John Davies acquired so much wealth that they were able to lend money to some of the Teifiside gentry, and also to the Bowens of Llwyngwair. James Bowen (1758-1816) borrowed £500 on 11 April 1807, from Thomas Davies, and this sum had not been repaid in the following June when the bond was assigned to John Davies. George Bowen (1800-56) signed bonds in May 1822 and in May and November 1830, each for £1,000. There was a connection with the Bowen family in that David, son of Thomas Davies, married Anna, daughter of the Reverend David Griffiths and his wife Anne, elder daughter of George Bowen, and when Thomas Davies died, David Griffiths conducted the burial service at St Mary's Church, Cardigan.

Captain John Davies died in 1835 and his will shows that he owned a house in Goat Street, together with other dwellings and land at Newport; two store houses, a coal-house and a smithy on the Parrog; land and dwellings at St Dogmael's, and the Red Lion Inn and some houses in

Cardigan, apart from shares in the brigs *Valiant, Mars, Mary and Eleanor, Minerva* and *Ocean*, the schooners *Thetis, Brothers, Martha and John*, the smack *Mary*, and the sloops *Aeron* and *Princess Royal*.

He left only two surviving sons. Llywelyn had gone down with the *Albion;* John was believed to have been drowned when his ship, the *Margaret*, sank returning from the Baltic in 1830, and David, with his crew, on the *Alert* in the same year. Evan, who had married and gone to live at Fishguard, had died in unknown circumstances some time before 1827. The beneficiaries in his will included his daughters Margaret, wife of William Roberts, and Ann, by then the widow of Captain David James of Newport, who had drowned when his ship, the *Elizabeth and Mary*, sank in 1828. Thomas (b 1807) was left a farm and an annuity of £10 a year, and William (b 1810), the youngest son, was given the business on the Parrog. He died four years later, however, and on 13 December 1839 a sale of his effects and shipping interests was held at the Castle Inn, Newport, and 'on the Parrog at the Storehouse lately occupied by the deceased.' Under the hammer went all his property, together with his inheritance of the seventh share in the twelve vessels left in his father's will.

Ships listed by Dr J Geraint Jenkins in his book *Maritime Heritage*[43] as 'belonging' to Newport, between 1770 and 1860, but built elsewhere, included:

Adena, schooner 84 tons built at New Quay 1825
Cambria, sloop 25 tons built Abercastle 1793.
Castle Malgwyn, sloop 100 tons built Cardigan 1800.
Commerce, sloop 35 tons built Carmarthen 1800.
Eliza, sloop 16 tons built Berkeley, Glos., 1822.
Eliza, schooner 160 tons built Milford 1827.
Excel, brig 213 tons built Milford 1854.
Exley, sloop 29 tons built Hull 1840.
Fly, sloop 23 tons, built 1860.
Frances, sloop 33 tons built Aberporth 1808.
Hope, brig 155 tons built Swansea 1813.
Hopewell, sloop 18 tons built New Quay 1810.
Jane & Catherine, sloop 29 tons built Conway 1837.
Jane & Marqaret, sloop 24 tons built Llansanffraid, Denb 1859.
John, sloop 89 tons built Milford Haven 1770.
John, schooner 70 tons built Bridgwater 1777.
John, sloop 28 tons built Milford 1828.
Margaret, snow 128 tons built Milford 1830.
Maria, schooner 64 tons built New Quay 1849.
Mary & Eliza, sloop 129 tons built Carmarthen 1824.
Neptune, smack 32 tons built Bristol 1827.
Oak, flat 33 tons built Queensferry 1840.
Pheasant, sloop 25 tons built New Quay 1837.
Price Jones, flat 23 tons built Flint 1859.
Prince Regent, sloop 31 tons built Solva 1813.
Richard & Mary, smack 18 tons built Pembroke Dock 1848.
Royal Recovery, brig 82 tons built Kidwelly.

76

Sarah, schooner 124 tons built Cardigan 1842.
Speculator schooner 76 tons built Aberystwyth 1804.
Tit Bit, brigantine 133 tons built Bridport 1849.
Twenty Two, sloop 31 tons built Cardiff 1822.

A record of some of the vessels that used to trade at Newport from 1876 to 1898 was published by Vincent Morris in the *County Echo* in 1958,[44] and among them were:

1876	*Ann and Betsy,* smack, 15 tons.	Miss Eliz Berriman.
	Price Jones, flat, 23 tons.	Thomas Roach.
1877	*Margaret Ellen,* smack 27 tons.	Thomas Davies.
1878	*Martha Jane,* smack, 17 tons.	John Jones.
1879	*Lerry,* smack, 33 tons.	Morris Davies.
1884	*New Providence,* smack, 32 tons.	Jacob Beer.
1885	*Albion,* dandy, 46 tons.	James Deeble.
1886	*Glyndwr,* schooner, 26 tons.	J Williams.
1895	*Cymro,* ketch, 28 tons.	J Williams.

Ships bringing commodities other than coal, culm and limestone during the same period included:

1876	*Jedulous,* schooner, 67 tons, taking 56 days to bring a load of 'manure and powder' from London.
	Favourite, 34 tons, bricks and ware from Chester.
	Spread Eagle, 26 tons, salt from Gloucester.
1877	*Rechabite,* 18 tons, superphosphate from Milford.
	George Evans, 32 tons, bricks from Bridgwater.
1878	*Eliza Anne,* 31 tons, freestone from Bristol.
1883	*Kate,* 25 tons, barley from Milford.
	Mountain Maid, 25 tons, salt from Gloucester.
1884	*Margaret Alice,* 26 tons, barley and manure from Milford.
	Tivyside, 62 tons, general cargo from Cardigan.
1885	*Albatross,* 28 tons, bricks and earthenware from Chester.
1891	*Mary,* 21 tons, load of sundries from Cardigan.
1893	*New Providence,* 32 tons, general cargo from Swansea.

The first steamer to enter the port was the *Sea Flower,* 62 tons, that called at Newport in October 1888 to discharge five tons of guano before proceeding, with its general cargo, from Cardigan to Bristol. The following month a steam tug-boat called, on its way from Liverpool to Cardiff, having run out of coal.

In June 1890, the yawl *Berthon* called on an experimental voyage in ballast from Southampton to Liverpool. It was a collapsible canvas boat, 28 ft long and 8 1/2 ft beam and 4 ft. deep and weighing about a ton, 'that will close to 13 inches [sic] for stowage'. It belonged to Messrs. Berthon & Co., of Romsey.

The onset of a sudden storm in summer drove the *Gauntlet* to seek shelter in the harbour on the evening of 31 July 1878. A schooner of 109 tons, master John Selby, with a crew of five, she carried a load of pig iron from Barrow to Rotterdam. The *Kitten*, 41 tons, owned by the River Plate Meat Co., London, on the other hand, was windbound, and with her machinery out of order, when she called, in ballast, on her way from Glasgow, in August 1886. The *Thomond*, arriving with a cargo of coal for the Cardigan Co-operative Society's depot on Parrog Road in August 1912, caught fast in the rocks while being piloted up-river and several tons of coal had to be discharged before she was able to re-float and be beached on the Parrog the next day.

A number of shipwrecks have taken place in, or in the vicinity of, Newport Bay. Those listed in *Welsh Shipwrecks*, by Tom Bennett, include the sloop *Jenny* (1840), the sailing ship *Lively* (1849), the sloop *Oak* (1861), the smack *Royal Oak* (1865), the *Jane and Margaret* (1879), and the schooner *Reliance* (1889).

More than one ship was driven on to the sands. On 17 March 1863, the sloop *Francis* of Cardigan was swept before a northerly gale on to Traeth Mawr and the crew of three were in danger of being washed overboard, but two local men, George Lewis and Thomas Rowlands, waded out through the breakers and managed to throw them a line. They were rewarded with the RNLI Silver Medal. The *Desdemona* of Aberystwyth ran ashore with a cargo of china clay on the Blackmares on 11 February 1906, during a gale that swept away the Fishguard lighthouse, but the crew was saved by the Newport Rocket Life-Saving Apparatus waggon which the Board of Trade had provided a fortnight earlier to replace the two-wheeled handcart that had been used hitherto.

The Life Saving Apparatus failed to save the lives of the crew of the *Oline*, a Danish schooner, on a wild night in March 1882. She had signalled that she was in distress off Dinas Head and the Fishguard lifeboat had set out, but had been unable to reach her on account of the ferocity of the gale and had to make for Cwmyreglwys. At dawn she was sighted having struck the rocks below Pen Catman. The Newport Life Saving Team got to the clifftop above and fired rockets. but the lines became entangled in the rigging and the crew of five perished almost within reach of land.

The tragedy led to a demand for a lifeboat and Mrs Leavington, of Clevedon, Somerset, who had been on holiday in Newport and had witnessed the death by drowning of a father and son when their yacht overturned, offered £1,000 for the provision of a lifeboat and the building of a lifeboat-house at Cwm. On 27 May 1884, the new lifeboat was launched from its new lifeboat house by Miss Bowen of Llwyngwair and named *The Clevedon*. The 37ft self-righting boat, propelled by six pairs of oars and a sail, had been built at a cost of £340. In the next five years it was called out only three times. but it saved eleven lives.

It was launched for the last time on 7 October 1889 when the brigantine *Reliance* of Wexford had her masts carried away in a gale and one of her crew washed overboard. The coxswain, William James, brought the lifeboat alongside the ship, to the north of Morfa Head, and took off the three surviving members of the crew, but the sea conditions were such that *The Clevedon* could not return and had to make for Cardigan.

The lifeboat station continued to function until 1895 when it was abandoned owing to the difficulty of launching the lifeboat, which could only be done at high tide.

Moorings for the safety of vessels visiting the port were constructed in 1914 through the joint efforts of Sir Marteine Lloyd, Sir George Bowen and the mayor and corporation.

In addition to the enduring perils of the sea, mariners had to face being overwhelmed by enemy vessels in times of war, and the permanent hazards of brigandage and piracy. Ships were sometimes lured to their fate by wreckers, and the plunder of a wrecked ship was common. When the *Two Partners*, owned by Llywelyn Evan, mariner, of Newport, foundered in Lydstep Bay in 1762, at the next Great Sessions, five men from that neighhourhood were charged with stealing from her cargo.

The ports of Pembrokeshire began to decline with the arrival of the railway in the county in the 1850's, but its failure to reach Newport enabled the coastal trade to continue there after it had ceased elsewhere. Throughout the nineteenth century the little ships brought their cargoes, and it was not until the arrival of road transport, with lorries delivering to the door, that coastal trading came to an end.

In 1884, ninety-seven vessels visited the port, but the numbers declined thereafter, although more than fourteen hundred vessels had unloaded their cargoes there during the last quarter of the century.

For a small boy in the 1920's, it was a tremendous thrill to see the tips of the masts of a ketch or a schooner appear below Pen Catman, waiting for the tide, and to hear the barking commands of the pilot as he guided her along the channel to her berth in the harbour. When the tides were high the vessel would tie up alongside the wall by Camelot, which is built

Sailors to be.

on the site of one of the storehouses on Parrog Bach, but at neap tides, the ship would be beached on the Parrog.

Among the last vessels to trade were the *Newland,* a ketch owned by Jacob Beer, the *Thomond* (130 tons) owned and skippered by Captain George, Trefin; the *Harparees* (200 tons) a wooden steam barge built at Sittingbourne in 1920, owner and master Captain Rees, and wrecked in 1929; the *Traly* (150 tons) owner and master Captain Rees; the ketch *Garlandstone* (120 tons) built at Calstock, on the Tamar, for Captain John Russan of Dale in 1929, now owned by the National Museum of Wales and berthed at Porthmadoc, and the *Mary Jane Lewis* built by James Evans of Milford in 1899, which over-wintered on Traeth Cocs in 1927-28 and was left in the charge of a bos'un, called Jack, who regaled small boys with tales of the sea, and taught them to smoke cigarettes. The vessel finally became a skeleton on Angle beach.

The last ships to be locally owned were the *Anne* (30 tons) owned by David Luke, and the *Wave* (130 tons) belonging to J O Vaughan, which sank under its last master, Walter Varney, in the early 1930's. The last shipment to arrive at the port was a cargo of coal brought by the *Agnes* of Bideford in September 1934.

The prosperity of the port may be gathered from the existence of no less than five public houses. On the Parrog were the *Queen's Head,* where Morfan is now, the *Sloop Inn* (Beach View), the *Parrog Arms* (Morawelon) and the *Ship Afloat* (Seagull Cottage), and beyond Bettws stood the *Mariner's Arms.*

Little evidence of that thriving time remains. The slate quay walls are its memorials, and the limekiln that escaped the vandals. The last storehouse survives as the Newport Boat Club.

A lone sailor once gave expression to his *hiraeth* in a simple sea shanty that was lost, and found again when it was heard, by a mariner from Dinas, being sung during the discharging of a ship at New Orleans. The author used the shanty, a copy of which had been given to him by Jack Francis, then head-teacher at Dinas, in a broadcast programme and, as it had only one verse, he wrote another in the same vein. It was sung by the local baritone, Mansel Owen, and, in a later programme, by Grace Nevern. It was also included in the repertoire of Cantorion Ingli, who recorded it in a medley of songs.

The song, sung to the tune *Ffarwel i Ddociau Lerpwl,* calls for 'the first to get down to the Parrog, to see the seventy-four (gunner): her bows are on the castle, her stern is on the shore. Farewell, the strands of Pembrokeshire! Farewell, the merry maidens! I go without delay, to sail upon the sea. O Mari, come with me. The breeze has stirred: it fills the white sheet'.

Am y cynta' i lawr i'r Parrog
I weld y "Seventy-Four",
Mae'i bows hi ar y Castell
A'i starn hi ar y môr.
Ffarwel i draethau Penfro
A'r merched ifainc llon;
'Rwy'n mynd yn awr heb oedi
I nofio ar y don.

O dewch, Mari,
I forio ar y llyn;
Mae'r awel wedi codi
I lanw'r lliain gwyn.

Ffarwel hen Afon Nyfer,
Ffarwel fy mam a nhad,
Mae'r awydd wedi codi
Ymado wnaf â'm gwlad.
Ffarwel i dŵr Carningli,
Ffarwel i'r bwthyn bach;
Ffarwel i'r merched perta',
Rwy'n awr yn canu'n iach.

ROADS AND TRANSPORT

The inhabitants of north Pembrokeshire had to rely on the sea for their communication with the outside world until comparatively recent times. It was not until 1771 that an act was obtained to extend 'the great London road' beyond Tavernspite to Hakin and Pembroke to meet the growth of road traffic in the second half of the eighteenth century, and another twenty years were to pass before a bill was introduced in Parliament to establish a trust that would take over the roads from Haverfordwest to Maenclochog, and to St Davids and along the coast to Fishguard and Newport and Cardigan. The trust was only granted to the Haverfordwest to Fishguard road, and the others remained free of the turnpike trusts. The Whitland Trust, that was responsible for the road running westward from St Clears to join the Tavernspite Trust road at Robeston Wathen, had roads running north, that were known as the lime roads, as limestone was carried along them from south Pembrokeshire to feed the limekilns in the north of the county.

Evan Jones observed, in 1890[1] that 'middle-aged people remember the time when the first public conveyance between Newport and the outer world was started. This was an omnibus run through the town from Cardigan to Milford, a Mr Charles being its proprietor as well as driver. A Mr Partridge soon followed with another omnibus on alternate days. These omnibuses, were driven along this route for many years, taking the Newport mariners to Milford, who thence went by steamer to Liverpool and other places.'

A coach service was provided by Messrs Cummins, Weston and Parker to run between Cardigan and Aberystwyth in June 1852, and the same firm ran a coach from Cardigan via Newport and Fishguard to Haverfordwest and Milford three days weekly each way.[2] When that service ceased, 'the North Mail, whose headquarters is at the Llwyngwair Arms', was running between Newport and Haverfordwest.[3]

The railway reached Carmarthen in 1852, and it was extended westward to Narberth Road (Clunderwen), Clarbeston Road and Haverfordwest by the end of 1853, and then on to Neyland and Milford. The Whitland and Taf Railway company was formed to build a railway to Cardigan but the line had only reached Crymych Arms by 1875, and it took another eleven years before it arrived at Cardigan. There had been proposals, as early as 1836, for the development of Newport as a port terminal and railhead, and in 1856 an effort. was made by the Court Leet and Thomas Davies Lloyd and, later by the Member of Parliament, James Bowen of Llwyngwair, to extend the railway from Cardigan to Newport and Fishguard.[4]

After the railway had reached Clarbeston Road in 1853, 'two-wheeled covered vans' were driven from Newport twice a week to that station and, from 1858, a coach known as *Y Cymro* was run by James Thomas from the Commercial (Castle) Hotel via Fishguard to Haverfordwest every Tuesday,[5] Thursday and Saturday at 6 a.m., and returning every Monday, Wednesday and Friday. In 1860, a poster[6] appeared to inform the public that John Williams's 'well-horsed omnibus will leave the Royal Oak Inn every morning, Sunday excepted, at 7 a.m., to meet the

Cardigan Omnibus at Crymmych Arms, and reach Narberth Road station in time for the 11.30 train' for London. The omnibus was named *The Regulator* and it ran until the railway station was open at Crymych. In 1880, a coach left the Commercial Hotel every day for Crymych. 'returning the same afternoon'. Another coach left the Llwyngwair Arms daily for Rosebush, and *The Express* left there for Haverfordwest, both returning the same night.

By 1920, 'a conveyance' left the Royal Oak at 7.45 a.m. daily for Crymych, and another at 8 a.m., except Wednesday, for Cardigan. The conveyance to Fishguard and Goodwick left the Post Office daily at 9.30 a.m. and 1.30 p.m.

The most celebrated conveyance was *Y Shah,* owned by Mr Jackson of the Prince of Wales Inn and later sold to Captain Davies of the Commercial (now the Castle) Hotel which travelled daily between Newport and Crymych. It was the subject of a popular ballad by the Reverend John Jones (Ioannes Towy): 'Hark, the post-horn blows; *Y Shah* is on its way from lovely Newport to fair Crymych to meet the "fire-horse" there, and then return through a scenic countryside, through Eglwyswrw and Felindre and along the river Nevern, until the sea comes into sight and the post-horn blows to announce the return to Newport. The sailor, home from the sea with his family, has but a short stay before he goes again with *Y Shah,* on his way to Liverpool to join his ship. May God be with him, sailing on his voyage towards Heaven!'   Mrs. Anne Hughes-Rees, who died in 1990 in her 102nd year, informed the author that she had travelled in *Y Shah,* taking her father back to sea, on its last run to Crymych in 1892. James Thomas Isaac told the author, in 1952, that he remembered the coach, and that the post-horn was a man named Thomas Jenkins. He was able to recite most of the verses:

Mae'r corn yn bloeddio, Beth sy'n bod?
Y Shah, y cerbyd mawr, sy'n dod,
Ar bedair o olwynion cryf
Yn llusgo llwythi trwm yn hyf.

Mor hardd, mor nerthol yw *Y Shah!*
Mor gyflym ac mor ddewr yr a!
O Drefdraeth fwyn i Grymych lân
Y rhed i gwrdd a'r cerbyd tân.

A chluda deithwyr ar eu taith
I ddwr y môr o bellter maith;
Saeson, Cymry, iach a chlaf
Ddônt gyda'r Shah ar ddydd o haf.

A golygfeydd rhyfeddol iawn
Ar hyd y ffordd i gyd a gawn;
Bryniau, coedydd, a dolydd gwyrdd,
A rhyfeddodau anian fyrdd.

Trwy Eglwyswrw y mae'n hardd,
Ac yn Velindre mae fel gardd;
Swynol a hyfryd yw mewn gair,
O Grymych fryniog i Lwyngwair.

Ar fin y ffordd y Nevern lân
Ymdreigla tua'r môr ymla'n;
Glwys afon loew enwog yw,
Ar fin yr hon fu Tegid fyw.

Bloedded yr udgorn megis cawr,
A'r môr yn dod i'r golwg 'nawr;
I'r preseb yr â y ddau farch da,
A boed llonyddwch heno i'r Shah.

Y morwr wedi teithio'r byd
Ddaw gyda'r Shah mewn llawen fryd,
I weld y tŷ a'i wraig a'r plant
Fu ar ei gof amserau gant.

Ac O'r llawenydd sydd gerllaw;
Cusanu, gwenu ac ysgwyd llaw,
Y morwr wedi dod yn iach
I ail gofleidio ei rai bach.

Meddyliodd am eu gwedd a'u hynt
Pan ar y môr mewn stormydd gwynt,
Myfyriai ef am danynt hwy
Pan ruthra'r storom eto'n fwy.

Pan cwyd y môr eiu donnau mawr
Yn ddŵr fynyddau hyll eu gwawr,
Fe gofia'r morwr y pryd hyn
Am wraig ei fron a'i blentyn gwyn.

Pan 'nol i'r môr y morwr â,
Rhaid cychwyn eto gyda'r Shah,
Rhaid codi'n fore gyda'r wawr
I wynebu tua Lerpwl Fawr.

Ti forwr hwylus fron,
Duw fo'th Dad ar frig v don;
Bydd dithau'n ufudd iddo Ef
Tra 'n morio ar dy daith i'r Nef.

IOANNES TOWY

The first reference to a bridge at Newport is contained in Nicholas
Martin's charter of c1278 in which he states that the rights of pasture
granted to the burgesses extended to 'the marshland on both sides of the

river called Nevern as far as the bridge of the town of Newport over the Nevern'. The rental of 1583, referring to a decayed mill, stated that it was situated 'a little above Newport Bridge by St Curig's chapel' and the bridge is mentioned again in the extent of 1594 and, in his *Taylor's Cussion* (1599),[7] George Owen notes in 1598, that Newport Bridge had six arches and was built of stone, whereas the bridges at Nevern and Cardigan and at Llechryd were of timber.

There was a belief that the bridge had been demolished by the townspeople because they thought that 'the sweating sickness' that had decimated their numbers in the sixteenth century had been carried by the inhabitants of the Morfa Quarter, on the other side of the river. The people from that area, therefore, had to use the stepping stones to cross the river except at high tide, when they would have to call, or whistle, for a boat to row them across. The boat was operated for many years by Elizabeth Griffiths, and her sister Hannah, who lived in the cottage nearest the river at Pen-y-bont. Elizabeth was born in 1835 and, by her own account, she had rowed the ferry boat from the time she was able to row until the new bridge was opened.

The proposal to build a bridge materialized with the formation of 'the Penbont Bridge Committee',[9] the first recorded meeting of which took place in January 1891 with the Mayor, Thomas James Davies, in the chair. Reports were received from 'gentlemen appointed to canvass the neighbourhood for subscriptions' towards building a bridge at an estimated cost of £1,400. They showed that £735 had been promised, £566 of which was from the parish of Nevern, £20 from Moylegrove, and £148 from Newport. Dr David Havard, the County Councillor for Newport, was requested to ask the Pembrokeshire County Council for 'a sum not exceeding £700 ... on condition that a similar sum be provided

Stepping stones used before Newport Bridge was built, 1894.

85

by private subscriptions and that the Bridge be taken over for future maintenance by the County.'

At the next meeting, held on 13 February, the Mayor was also appointed Secretary to the committee. It was reported that the County Council had approved the proposal to build the bridge and had agreed to contribute up to £700 towards the cost of its erection, and it was then decided to advertise for tenders and to dig trial holes. On 3 April, the committee considered the only tender received, from Messrs. Clifford and Sampson Morgan, Back Lane, Haverfordwest, 'for the completion of the masonry, earthwork, metalling, pitching, etc.,' in the sum of £695. Messrs Pierson and Co., Fenchurch Street, London, were to provide the ironwork, comprising girders and iron lattice parapet railings, for £220, and Thomas Johns, timber merchant, of Cardigan, was to convey the ironwork fron Cardigan, or Boncath, GWR station at fifteen shillings per ton. His men were to be 'allowed two or three pints of Beer, as advisable,' after the delivery of the whole consignment.

The committee met every week, at the Justices' Room, but there were not enough members present to form a quorum on 11 December, nor on the 18th., or on Christmas Day or New Year's Day! The work was to be completed by 30 October 1891, but there were delays and the final payment was not made to Messrs Clifford and Sampson Morgan until 30 September 1892.

It was unanimously resolved, on 7 October 1892, that any balance remaining, after all payments had been made, 'be handed over to the Secretary in acknowledgement of the indefatigable and zealous services rendered by him in furthering the work to its completion and collecting the monies, etc.'

On 13 January 1893, Major-General Charles S Sturt, of Newport Castle, who had been appointed mayor the previous November, became chairman in succession to T J Davies. The County Council had not remitted the £700, although its payment had been approved on 7 November 1892 and, on 28 July, the Council was requested to forward this amount, together with a sum not exceeding £35 'to meet expenses caused by delay in payment'.

On 31 August 1893 it was reported 'that horned cattle and heavy draught horses' had been seen clambering up the slopes, and on to the bridge, causing damage. Mr J B Bowen of Llwyngwair stated that he would place a railing on 'the Nevern side of the river, if another were placed on the Newport side,' and this was done.

The thirty-third and final meeting was held on 14 March 1894 at 3.30 p.m. A balance sheet was produced by the Secretary and the 'guarantee sheet to Messrs Lloyds, Ltd., bankers, Cardigan for a sum not exceeding £1,400' was destroyed. The balance in hand, amounting to £25, was presented to T J Davies, as previously agreed, 'in recognition of the great and valuable services rendered by him ... to bring matters to a successful issue, which has been done in a most satisfactory manner.'

CHURCH AND CHAPELS

ST. MARY'S CHURCH

The church was built by William Martin after he had established himself at Newport Castle in the early years of the thirteenth century.

The twelfth century 'Life of Brynach'[1] states that a church had been built 'at the foot of the mountain .... called *Mons Angelorum*', that is, Carn Ingli, and it has been suggested that the reference could have been to an earlier church that was dedicated to St Curig. There was a chapel to which George Owen refers as 'St Kiricke's chapel at a place called in owd tyme Millbrook',[2] a little above Newport Bridge, and near it is a well called Ffynnon Gurig. Owen also refers to 'a greate faire' that was held on St Curig's Day which, he said, was the 16th of June.[3]

Curig is a saint of unrecorded genealogy who died before the turn of the sixth century, and he is referred to as Curig Lwyd (The Blessed Curig), and also as Curig Farchog (Curig the Knight).[4] He has been confused with Cyriacus, the child saint from Asia Minor who was killed, with his mother, Julitta, or Ilid, during the persecution of the Christians by Diocletian in 304 AD, and whose feast day is 16th June whereas that of St Curig is 17th February.

As it was the Norman custom to re-dedicate churches to Roman saints, it is possible that Curig was abandoned in favour of the Virgin Mary. In Carmarthenshire, Eglwys Fair a Churig retains the dual dedication. Curig is also remembered at Capel Curig, in Snowdonia, and also at Llangurig and nearby Eisteddfa Gurig (Curig's Seat), at the foot of

Newport Castle, St Mary's Church and Church Chapel.

Pumlumon. Richard Fenton stated that Ffos y Mynach (the Monk's Dyke), in the parish of St David's, was also known as Ffos Gurig.[5]

A legend states that Curig was an Irishman[6] and that when he was at Eglwys Fair a Churig he killed his fellow-saint, Gwinio, who had a settlement at nearby Llanwinio and that he then thought it 'prudent to withdraw to a less dangerous region'.[7] He went to Newport.

During the Middle Ages the church, and the churchyard, were also used for secular purposes.[8] The church was normally sited towards the northern boundary of a churchyard, and the area surrounding it remained unconsecrated, while the southern part would be sanctified as a place for burials. The unhallowed ground was used by the parishioners for holding markets and patronal feasts, and for playing games and pastimes. In bad weather they resorted to the nave of the church, which was also not consecrated. Evan Jones (1890)[9] states that 'within the memory of the oldest inhabitants the Church tower at Newport, as at many other places, was much used to play ball (chwareu pêl), the favourite game at that time. It is said that great matches were frequently played, and that the ball was often thrown over the steeple. Sometimes it would be thrown on the roof of the so-called Record Office adjoining the steeple, causing much trouble and annoyance to the players; and sometimes on the roof of the steeple itself, whence it could not be recovered except with the assistance of Shaki Shon Morgan, the sexton. Many a shilling did old Shaki make by selling the balls he found on the steeple. Good old John Thomas, the present sexton, derives no benefit from this kind of perquisite, for ball-playing has been discontinued for many years past.'

The 'so-called Record Office' is mentioned by Samuel Lewis in his *Topographical Dictionary of Wales* (1848)[10] where he states that 'on the

J 'Warwick' Smith 1787.

west side of the porch are the ruins of a detached house said to have been the record office of the town'.

Only the tower remains of the original building erected in the early part of the thirteenth century.[11] Two escutcheons above the west door, according to Fenton, bore 'the same coat, (viz) Party per pale a chevron', which may be a misreading of the arms of Touchet, Lords Audley and lords of Cemais from 1405 to 1497, namely, *ermine* a chevron *gules*.[12] There are also shields to be seen on the north wall, and on either side of the west door, but none is decipherable. There are carved faces at the corners of the tower, except for the south-west, where it has been removed, and may be the one that appears on the north-west buttress above a holy water stoup.

An aquatint of 1787 by John 'Warwick' Smith shows the tower surmounted by a steeple that looked like a television aerial. It now has a splendidly defiant weathercock.

Three bells hang in the tower, one dated 1809, another 1812, while the third, having been cracked by over-ringing, was recast and is inscribed 'Victoria Jubilee 1887'.

The stone pillar in front of the west door provides the earliest evidence of Christianity in the parish. It dates from the seventh or eighth century and has an incised linear Latin ring-cross with crossleted foot and an upward curved short bar below.[13] It was discovered by Sir Mortimer Wheeler in 1924 when it served, head downwards, as a gatepost to a field opposite Cnwce farm, at the corner of which stood the gallows. When the field was being developed as a building site in 1953, the author had the stone removed, with the consent of the Inspectorate of Ancient Monuments and the Diocesan Board, to its present position. Another pillar-stone with an incised circle enclosing a linear cross with a dot in each interspace is said to have been found face-down in the churchyard, and is now in a nearby garden.

The earliest record of the church occurs in the *Taxatio* of 1291 where it is described as *Ecclesia de Novo Burgo* and 'assessed at £8 for tenths to the King'. In 1326, following the death of the last of the Martins, the advowson, of the yearly value of twelve marks. with other advowsons and knights' fees, were assigned to William Martin's nephew and coheir, James, Lord Audley, as the new lord of Cemais.

There may be reference to an early incumbent in Nicholas Martin's charter of about 1240, which was witnessed, among others, by '[Ho]welo ab Evan Meredith, cl[er]ico'. There was also 'John del Orchard, chaplein del chastel et le segno'ie de Newport in about 1364. Richard Caunton, cleric in 1381, became Archdeacon of Cardigan.[14]

William Peek, formerly rector of Dinas, was the incumbent in 1398.[15] On 17 November that year, he obtained a licence for non-residence for a year for the obsequies of Nicholas, Lord Audley and lord of Cemais. Walter Wall was granted a licence of non-residence on 12 March 1401 on condition that he gave £20 towards 'building the church and his mansion there'. The licence was cancelled shortly afterwards and Wall exchanged the living with John Porter, rector of Llanfair Nantygof, on 28 August 1402. Porter obtained a licence for non-residence for a year on 4 January 1406, and another on 31 March 1407. In 1410 he exchanged with David Fauconer the living of Wykham in the diocese of Rochester.

Thomas Devonald was rector in 1434, and in 1519 the incumbent was Thomas Kemeys. In his will, dated 7 April 1559, he directed that 'Sir Thomas ap Rotherike, my parish priest of Newport in Kemmeys' should by the oversight of Master Gwyn, archdeacon of Cardigan, receive all duties 'belonging to the parsonage of Newport, to pay my debts.'[15] In

Incised cross, 7th/8th century, in St Mary's churchyard.

1535, according to the *Valor Ecclesiasticus,* the rector was William Davies, and the office was held in 1572 by William Awbery.

In the extent of 1594 it is stated that the lord of Cemais 'is sole patrone of the church' and that it 'is valued in the queen's books to £16, but it is worth by the yeere 100 markes and Mr. Richard Edwardes, clercke, channceler of the cathedrall church of St Davides, ys now parson theare by the presantment of George Owen, esquior, now lord of the manor.'[16]

Richard Edwardes was appointed rector in 1583. He had been installed chancellor of the diocese in July 1571, and admitted canon-resident in September that year. He built Coedwynog, in the parish of Nevern, in 1588, and died there in 1600. His place as rector had been taken by John Lewis in 1594.

The 1594 extent records that 'to the saide rectorie there is a personage howse, beinge halfe a myle owte of the towne, which is called the Coorte, and to the same is there belonginge faire gleebe landes but ye house, stables, barnes and other buildings are ruinowse and decayed.'[17] A terrier, or 'Plan of the Glebe Lands belonging to Newport Church' of 1772 gives The Court as situated 'in a field at the extreme south-west corner of the Glebe' and Evan Jones states that 'the buildings were afterwards taken down and re-erected in the more convenient situation which they now occupy'.[18] He also recorded that in the rectory garden there lay 'a mutilated quern, or handmill' and added the speculation that as 'the tenants were bound by manorial deeds and feudal custom to take all grist to their lord's mill and to pay toll on the same', the use of handmills was illegal and any discovered would be broken and the owner punished.[19] The Court was sold in 1985 and a new rectory was established in the town.

Lewis Thomas, who graduated at Jesus College, Oxford, in July 1597, was the rector in 1600, but he removed to Robeston West in the following year.[20] He had previously been the schoolmaster at the College at Felindre Farchog, and witnessed deeds in that village in 1591 and 1594, when he was described as 'pedagog of Velindre'.[21]

Morgan Walter,[22] who had been born in 1581 and had matriculated at Queen's College, Oxford, was the rector from 1607 to 1610, when he moved to Llanddewi Velfrey. He was made a Canon of St David's in 1612.

Evan Owen, natural son of George Owen of Henllys, was presented to the living in 1623 by his brother, Thomas Owen of Wenallt. He had matriculated at Jesus College, Oxford, in the previous year, when he was twenty-one years of age. He became rector of Llanychlwydog in 1626, and of Walwyn's Castle in 1638, and was collated Chancellor of St David's Cathedral in 1644 and installed the following year.

In his will, dated 20 March 1628, James Bowen of Llwyngwair left £5 towards the repair of Newport church. His son, George Bowen, who died in 1659, left 5s. for the same purpose.

In 1638 William Williams was presented to the incumbency by George Owen, York Herald, on behalf of his half-brother, Alban Owen, lord of Cemais. Administration of his goods was granted at Carmarthen on 16 April 1672. On 1 October that year, Daniel Gwyn, B.A., was presented to the living by William Owen, lord of Cemais, who, in 1679, presented

John Parry. In 1685, Charles Price was presented by Thomas Corbet, Esq., of Ynysmaengwyn, presumably on behalf of his sister, Anne, the widow of David Owen, lord of Cemais, who had died leaving two daughters and coheirs, Elizabeth Laugharne of Llanrheithan, and Anne Lloyd of Penpedwast. John Bolton was presented to the living by Arthur Laugharne on 16 January 1700, and James Williams, M.A., was presented in his place, in 1714, by Anne Lloyd, widow. James Williams was succeeded, at his death in 1735, by William Laugharne, who was presented by John Laugharne of Llanrheithan.

Watkin Lewes, of Penybenglog, rector of Meline from 1735, was presented to the incumbency in 1759 by Thomas Lloyd of Bronwydd, lord of Cemais. His son, by his wife Ann Williams of Ambleston, was Sir Watkin Lewes, Lord Mayor of London in 1780-81 and Member of Parliament for the City of London from 1781 to 1796

Daniel Rowland, Llangeitho,[23] was offered 'the comfortable living of Newport' in 1769, by John Thornton, of Clapham to whom Thomas Lloyd had granted the next presentation of the rectory in consideration of a payment of £300, but he declined it. Had he accepted, Newport, and not Llangeitho, might have been 'the mecca of Methodism'.

David Pugh,[24] born at Dolgellau in 1739, and a graduate of Hertford College, Oxford, succeeded Watkin Lewes in 1770. He was sympathetic to the Methodists' cause and was described as 'the Methodistical rector of Newport'.[25] He was a frequent visitor to Llwyngwair, where he met John Wesley and other leading Methodists, and he was acquainted with the Moravian teacher, Benjamin le Trobe. When the movement towards separate ordination began, however, he changed his attitude and attacked its promoters. He died on 5 December 1816 and was buried in St Mary's churchyard.

It was during Pugh's incumbency in 1799, that the Church Chapel was built, and The Court re-erected. In 1811 the church needed repair and a Vestry Meeting agreed that a parish rate be levied to raise £30 for that purpose.

After Pugh's death in 1817, John Jones was presented to the living by Mary Lloyd of Bronwydd, widow of Colonel Thomas Lloyd, He did not take up residence and the church was served by a curate-in-charge. The curates[26] during this period were William Grey Hughes, who was appointed Vicar of Mathry in 1822 and died two years later and is commemorated by a tablet in the chancel, and David Davies, who was appointed to the rectory of Meline in 1824. Jones resigned that year and was presented to the living of Llangynllo, which was also in the gift of the Lloyds.

Llewelyn Lloyd Thomas, a native of Pencarreg, in Carmarthenshire, was presented by Mary Lloyd in 1824 and he was to hold the living for fifty-one years. He was appointed mayor in 1855-57 and appears to be the first rector to hold that office. The church was renovated in 1834-35 and a gallery built, by the local builder John Morgans. The Cambrian Archaeological Association, after its visit in 1859, reported that 'the church has undergone so many alterations that little remains of the original edifice.'[27]

Evan Jones who, like Thomas, was a native of Pencarreg, succeeded as rector in 1875 by the presentment of Sir Thomas Davies Lloyd, Bart. One of his first tasks was to renovate the church and The Court, where he added a cowshed and a cart-house to the existing buildings. He was made a Canon of St David's Cathedral and was mayor of Newport in 1890-91.

He considered the church to be 'one of the ugliest churches in Pembrokeshire. On the outside, the roof was flat and inside the church the pews were high and the pulpit, a kind of three-deck construction, the one rising above the others, was set in the middle of the chancel arch. I understood, even before I arrived,' he wrote in his *Deugain Mlynedd o Weinidogaeth* (Forty Years of Ministry), 'that one of my first, and most important, duties would be to renovate the parish church,'[28] and he followed the great vogue of the time of renovating and often destroying, the interior of country churches. He set up a committee in 1878, under the chairmanship of James Bevan Bowen of Llwyngwair, the Member of Parliament and a former mayor of Newport, which commissioned John Middleton of Cheltenham, who had renovated a number of churches in the area, to prepare plans, and William and David Evans of Cilgerran were appointed to carry out the work. The task was completed in sixteen months, at a cost of £2,580, and the church was re-dedicated by Bishop Basil Jones of St David's on 30 September 1879. 'The only portions of the original structure which still remains,' the rector was proud to say, 'are the tower, font, holy water stoup and rood-loft steps at the left-hand side of the chancel arch.'

The bare walls, of grey and brown igneous stone, highlight the stained glass windows. The east window has four lights, depicting the four Evangelists, Matthew, Mark, Luke and John, and it commemorates the former rectors, Llewelyn Lloyd Thomas and Evan Jones. It is by A O Hemming of London. Two small windows by Heaton, Butler and Bayne of London were placed in the sanctuary during the restoration, one in memory of John Morgan, who died in 1865 after serving for forty-seven years as master of Madam Bevan's Central School at College Square, and the other commemorating seventeen-year old Ida Marion Nicholas, of Spring Gardens, contains a medallion of the Nativity, that is said to be fourteenth century and Austrian in origin, and two other medallions presented by her mother, who was formerly married to the Rev John Evans, rector of Crickhowell.

There are three stained glass windows in the chancel and several memorial tablets, one of which commemorates Captain John Davies, who had established the shipping trade at Newport in the early part of the nineteenth century and had died in 1835, together with members of his family. Another tablet is to the memory of his grandson, Thomas Davies James, 'a young man of considerable promise as respects piety and attainment'.

In his 'List of Buildings having Mural Decoration' (1873), C. E. Keyser includes Newport as one of six churches in Pembrokeshire and apart from St. David's Cathedral, it was the only one in north Pembrokeshire.[29]

The nave is unusual in having twin-gabled transepts which are divided from the nave by arches of cream freestone. The south transept, dedicated as the Lady Chapel in 1976, has an altar piece by a local artist.

The Norman cushion-type font is regarded as one of the finest in the county. A medieval holy water stoup beside it only came to light when a gallery was removed during the 1879 restoration.

A fourteenth century coffin lid, unearthed by a gravedigger in the middle of the last century, has been mounted on a stone slab and lies in the vestry. It has a face in relief and a floriated cross, and the incomplete inscription:.... CES: ANE: GIT: ICI: DEV: DEL: ALME: EIT: MERCIE, commemorating a nameless one who 'lies here, may God have mercy on his soul.'[30]

The church plate[31] comprises an Elizabethan chalice, with paten cover and inscribed POCULUM * ECLESIE * DE * NEWPORTHE and the date 1574; another chalice and paten cover bearing the inscription 'Newport. A gift from the Communicants to the Parish 1826'; an ewer-shaped Flagon, hall-marked 1880 and inscribed 'To the Glory of God and in loving memory of Sarah Bowen who entered into rest 17th Sep 1874', which was presented by her daughter, Martha Margaret Bowen of Cotham Lodge. A Wafer Box was presented by their children in memory of the Rev D T Evans, rector 1967-73, and his wife.[32] It is said that small medieval chalices in the possession of the church were melted down, or sold, to provide the larger vessel, needed when the Cup was given to the laiety after the Reformation.

The churchyard was extended in 1886 by the addition of an adjoining field, of a quarter of an acre, that was part of the Glebe, and a wall was built around it. The cost was met by members of the church and of the chapels in the town, and the ground was consecrated by the Bishop of St. David's on 5 April that year.[33] Additional land was acquired in 1936. The need for a public cemetery had been expressed for some time when, in September 1921, the Newport Parish Council, at a special meeting, resolved to purchase a field on the Penfeidr road, above The Mount, for the sum of £135, which they laid out and named the Brynhyfryd Cemetery.

The Church Chapel was built in 1799[34] 'by the voluntary contributions of divers well disposed people' on land leased by George Bowen of Llwyngwair 'for the use, benefit and accommodation, and conveniency of the preaching the Holy Gospel and for a congregation to assemble for hearing Divine worship according to the doctrinal Articles and Homilies of the Established Church of England, and for assemblies or meetings for the purpose of reading the Holy Scriptures, praying, catechising and instructing in the principles of religion as contained in the said doctrinal Articles and Homilies, but for no other principles of religion whatsoever.' The Methodists, at that time, were full members of the church and were happily suffered, whatever their dissenting beliefs, and especially so at Newport where the rector, David Pugh, was sympathetic to their cause and willing to allow John Wesley to preach from his pulpit. Similar chapels were erected at Nevern, Eglwyswrw and St Dogmael's, following the example at Haverfordwest where the Wesley Room had been built beside St Martin's Church churchyard in 1772. It is not insignificant that the trustees of the Church Chapel included the incumbents of Nevern and St Dogmael's, and Essex Bowen of Llwyngwair.

The freehold of the Chapel and the adjoining cottage was acquired in

1877, and a garden 'situate near the saw-pit' was bought in 1889 for the use of the cottage. In the meantime, the cottage on the south side was purchased, and this has recently been demolished and a garden takes its place.

The Chapel was built on the lines of the barn-inspired design of early Welsh chapels, with the door on one side. It had box pews rising in tiers, with a pulpit and dais facing the doors. The seats have been removed and the Chapel has been adapted for present-day needs, and the adjoining cottage has been converted into a kitchen and toilets.

The Chapel is one of few places in Wales where the *Plygain* service is still observed on Christmas morning.[35] The service has its origins in the Midnight Mass held in Rome in the fifth century to which, in 431 AD. Pope Sixtus III added a stational Mass, and another was added to celebrate the birth of Christ. In the Sarum Missal, one of these Masses is called *Missa in gallicantu*, 'the mass held at cock-crow'. The word *plygain* is derived from the Latin *pulli cantus*, where *pullus* can mean 'a young cockerel', and there is no explanation for its use in this context. It is also a peculiarity that the derivative is written *plygain*, rather than *pylgain*, which is the way it is frequently pronounced. At Newport it is called *Y Bwlgen*.

The service continued, in a modified form, after the Reformation,[36] and it survived in many places up to the end of the last century, or later. Before the Reformation, the Mass was conducted entirely in Latin, but afterwards it became possible for community singing to develop in the form of hymns and carols.

It became the practice for Nonconformists also to attend the *plygain* service, which formerly commenced at five o'clock in the morning at Newport, and now begins at six. People of all denominations attend and take part in the service, which comprises readings from the Old and New Testaments, prayers and the singing of hymns without accompaniment. One of the hymns that is traditionally sung, with measured tones, at the service, is:

O angau pa le mae dy golyn?
O uffern, ti gollaist y dydd
Y Baban a aned ym Methlehem

A goncrodd pob gelyn a sydd.
Ni raid i blant Seion ddim ofni
Tra'n teithio i fyny tua'r wlad

Mae'r brif-ffordd yn rhydd i
fynd adre
Mae wedi'i phalmantu â gwaed.

Newport was at the southern edge of the district where *halsingod*[37] were written and sung. They were first defined by Erasmus Saunders in his *View of the State of Religion in the Diocese of St David's* in 1721, as

'a kind of Divine Hymns, or Songs, which they call *Halsingod*, or Carolion, which generally consist either of the Doctrinal, or Historical parts of the Scripture, or of the Lives, and worthy Acts of some eminent

Saints, ... [sung] at home ... at their Wakes and ... in their Churches in the Winter Season ... before and after Divine Service ... Eight or Ten will commonly divide themselves to Four or Five of a side, and ... one Party first begins, and then by way of Alternate Responses, the other repeats the same Stanza, and so proceed till they have finish'd their *Halsing,* and then conclude with a Chorus ... At the Feast of the Nativity ... they ... come to Church about Cock-crowing ... and then set themselves to sing the fore-mention'd *Halsingod.*'

The *halsingod* were written almost exclusively in the southern half of Cardiganshire and in Cemais between 1622 and 1750. Some forty authors of *halsingod* have been traced, two of them, David Michael and George Thomas, lived in the parish of Meline, and one, unknown by name, was from 'plwitreidreth' (the parish of Newport).

THE METHODISTS

The Methodist movement had its origin in a small religious society founded by Charles Wesley at Christ Church, Oxford, in 1729. It was known, mockingly, as 'the Holy Club', and it comprised, apart from Charles, his brother, John Wesley, George Whitefield and two others, until they were joined by John Gambold, a native of Puncheston. He soon left them to embrace Moravianism and became a bishop of that sect, while the Society developed into an evangelistic movement within the Church of England, from which it separated in 1791. Welsh Methodism had its roots in the conversion of Howell Harries when he heard the vicar of Talgarth deliver a Whitsuntide sermon during the Great Awakening of 1735. He came on a preaching tour of north Pembrokeshire four years later, and made thirty more visits, although a division eventually took place between him and the other Methodist leaders.

The patron of Methodism in north Pembrokeshire, George Bowen of Llwyngwair, was said to have been converted when he was passing through Trecastle in his carriage, and a young woman emerged from an evangelical meeting singing a hymn by William Williams, Pantycelyn,[38]. Bowen had trained in the law and had lived at Holmhouse until his father died in 1752, when he moved to Llwyngwair. He had already exchanged certain properties at Newport with Sir John Pakington, who had inherited the Perrot estate by marriage and, in 1756, he purchased further messuages and lands from him, including Trecadifor, Pant, Cerrig, Holmhouse and Dolrannog, at a total outlay of £7,700. His estate was considerably enlarged two years later when he married Easter, daughter of William Thomas of Pentowyn in the parish of Meidrim, who brought with her a halfshare of the Pentowyn and Castell Gorfod estates. Bowen furthermore acquired parts of the Wenallt estate and, by 1779, he was the owner of Berry Hill, that conveniently adjoined the Llwyngwair demesne. By 1806, however, he had overspent on land purchase and when he died, four years later, his son inherited debts amounting to £9,000.

William Williams, and other early Methodists, found an open house at Llwyngwair.[39] In his journal Williams stated that, on 2 September 1771, he and Daniel Rowland had travelled from Haverfordwest to Llwyngwair where they enjoyed the company of David Pugh, rector of Newport,[40] as well as that of the Bowen family. Williams preached 'to a vast audience in the open air', at Newport, on the Sunday evening. He referred, in a letter written in about 1786, to a *Sasiwn* held at Llwyngwair when 'Mr Bowen treated the whole Association. Hundreds of people, godly and ungodly, dined and were entertained. Sixty beds were occupied by strangers at Llwyngwair alone, and about six score sat down to meals there.[41]' He records that when he was there in 1790, he was 'ill of the gravel' and was 'obliged to rise 18 or 20 times out of bed each night, and often more', but this did not prevent him from preaching hour-long sermons at Newport and at Nevern. He, and other early Methodists, were able to preach at these churches as the parish priests, David Pugh and David Griffiths, were 'Methodistical clerics', sympathetic to the Methodist cause. David Griffiths, a native of Lampeter Velfrey, had come to Llwyngwair as tutor to the Bowen children and, in 1781, he married Anne, the eldest daughter. Two years later he was presented by the Crown to the living of Nevern, and he and his wife settled at Berllan near Eglwyswrw. In a letter of 1810, he stated that Berry Hill was 'about to be completed' and in March 1834, six years after his wife had died, he moved there, and he died there on 19 September that year, at the age of eighty, by his own hand.

William Williams is said to have been inspired, while at Llwyngwair, by the sight of Carn Ingli, in a glowering mood, as he looked out of his bedroom window, to write his famous hymn, 'O'er the gloomy hills of darkness....'[42]. The hymn was published in his book of English hymns, *Gloria in Excelsis,* and sung in all parts of the English-speaking world. It was translated into Welsh and became even more famous as 'Dros y bryniau tywyll niwlog...'

The Welsh Methodists regarded themselves more in harmony with the Calvinism of George Whitefield than the Arminianism of John Wesley and a gentleman's agreement was reached in 1747 whereby Whitefield would evangelise in Welsh Wales, and Wesley would only visit the English-speaking causes. Wesley made the first of fourteen visits to Pembrokeshire in 1763. He had Pembrokeshire connections in that he was the great-grandson, on the maternal side, of Griffith White of Henllan, in the parish of Rhoscrowther, and he had heard of George Bowen from a George Williams, of Pembroke, who had written to him stating: 'I am desired to inform you of a gentleman in the upper part of this county who has expressed an earnest desire of seeing you at his home and having you to preach in the neighbourhood, and it is much to be wished that you could comply with the request. He is a man of large property and resides within a few miles of the town of Cardigan. This gentleman, whose name is Bowen, contributed handsomely to the building in Haverfordwest.' The 'building' was 'the Wesley Room', later the Wesleyan Chapel, adjoining St Martin's churchyard, at the opening of which, on 18 August 1772, Wesley preached a sermon. Two days later he made the first of seven visits to Llwyngwair and, on most of these occasions, he preached at Newport, as recorded in his journal:

THURSDAY, 20 [August 1772]. I rode over [from Haverfordwet] to

Mr Bowen's at Llwyngwair, an agreeable place and an agreeable family. Here I rejoiced to meet Mr Pugh, whose living [at Newport] is within a mile of Llwyngwair. In the evening he read prayers at Newport and preached to a deeply serious congregation. I trust his lot is cast for good among a people both desirous and capable of instruction.

FRIDAY, 21. I preached about eight and then rode back to Haverfordwest.[43]

MONDAY, 14 [July 1777]. Reached Llwyngwair about noon. In the evening Mr Pugh read prayers and I preached at Newport. This is the only town in Wales which I had then observed to increase. In riding along on the side of Newport bay I observed on the ground a large quantity of turfs. These are found by removing the sand above high-water mark, under which there is a continued bed of turf with the roots of trees, leaves, nuts and various kinds of vegetables. So that it is plain the sea is an intruder here and now covers what was once dry land. Such probably was this whole bay a few centuries ago. Maybe it is not at all improbable that formerly it was dry land from Aberystwyth to St David's Point.

TUESDAY, 15. Mr Bowen carried me in his chaise to Cardigan...

WEDNESDAY, 16. About nine I preached again at Newport church and found much liberty among that poor simple people. We dined with Admiral Vaughan at Trecwn... [44]

SATURDAY, 27 [September 1777], ...I took chaise with Mr Goodwin and made straight for Mr Bowen's at Llwyngwair, in Pembrokeshire, hoping to borrow his sloop and so cross over to Dublin without delay.... The next day, October 1st, the captain of a sloop at Fishguard, a small seaport town ten or twelve miles from Llwyngwair, sent me word he would sail for Dublin in the evening, but he did not stir till about eight the next evening. We had a small fair wind....[45]

WEDNESDAY 18 [August 1779]. I preached about ten at Newport church and then we went to Haverfordwest.... [46]

FRIDAY, 4 [May 1781]. About eleven I preached at Newport church and again at four in the evening.

WEDNESDAY 18 [August 1784]. I went to Admiral Vaughan's at Trecwn, one of the pleasantest seats in Britain....

THURSDAY, 19. *4, prayed, letters; 8, prayer, tea, conversed; 9.15, chaise, visited; 12.30, Ll[wy]ngwair; 2.30, dinner, conversed; 4, prayed, tea, Matt. vii, 16, 6. supper together, prayer, hymns.* I went on to Mr Bowen's at Llwyngwair, another agreeable place, the more so because of the company — Mr and Mrs Bowen, his brother, and six of their eleven children, two of whom are lately come from the University.

FRIDAY, 20. *4, prayed, letter; 7, Rom. viii, 3-4, tea, conversed, chaise,*
Newport, prayers; 9, I Sam. xxi, 8; 9.30, chaise; 11.15, [Little]
New[castle], Jo. ii, 12; chaise, Hav[erfordwest], within dinner, visited many,
tea, Prayer; 6.30, Jo. iv, 24, supper, prayer. About eight I preached in the
Church at Newport and spoke strong words, if haply some might awake
out of sleep. Thence we went to Haverfordwest, it being the day when the
bishop held his visitation.

THURSDAY, 19 [August 1788]. A servant of Mr Bowen's came [to
Carmarthen] early in the morning to show us the way to Llwyngwair. and
it was well he did for I do not know that we could otherwise have found
our way thither. We met (as expected) with a hearty welcome. At five I
preached in Newport church to a large congregation and with a greater
prospect of doing good than ever I had before. We passed an agreeable
evening at Llwyngwair.

TUESDAY, 10 [August 1790]. *4, prayed, tea; 5, chaise; 10, tea, within;*
11, chaise; 1.30, Llwyngwair, writ journal; 2.30, dinner, conversed, letters:
tea, chaise with Mrs B[owe]n; 6, prayers, Prov. iii, 17; 7.30, chaise, prayer,
supper, conversed.

The Methodist movement remained within the Anglican Church, and
found no reason to do otherwise in view of the sympathetic attitude of
Edward Smallwell, Bishop of St David's, and of the local clergy at
Newport and Nevern. Samuel Horsley, when he was appointed bishop in
1788, adopted a different attitude, however, and complained of the
Methodists' 'disorderly zeal', and dissension grew generally between the
Methodist leaders and the clergy.

The sacrament was administered in a non-consecrated church for the
first time by the Reverend Howel Davies, curate of Llys-y-fran, 'the
Apostle of Pembrokeshire', at the opening of the Woodstock Chapel in
1755. The Methodists did not have any ordained ministers until 1811,
and one of the thirteen then ordained was Evan Harries, son of John
Harries of Ambleston, one of the Methodist exhorters, who died and was
buried at Newport in 1788.

Meetings were believed to have been held at the house of one John
Lloyd at Newport since 1743 and, in 1799, the Church Chapel was built,
for the use of Methodists and non-Methodists alike. When the
Methodists seceded from the established church, in 1811, the Church
Chapel was no longer available to them and they built their own chapel,
Tabernacle, in Long Street. The chapel was rebuilt in 1838, and again
in 1904. In 1873 the congregation appointed George Morgan its first
minister.

THE INDEPENDENTS

The little chapel at Brynberian, hidden among trees and surrounded by
laburnums, in the bosom of the Presely Hills, was the first established
home of the Independent cause in north Pembrokeshire.[47]

A catalogue of the 'congregational churches' in Wales in 1675 confirmed that there was, in Pembrokeshire, 'a small community lately gathered into church order by Mr James Davies,' who had been ejected from the living of Merthyr, near Carmarthen, in 1662, and that it met at the house of Captain Jenkin Jones, himself a teacher among them, at Cilgerran. It is further stated that most of these people were 'in church order before, being gathered originally by Mr Charles Price, who was their pastor,' and who had been ejected from Cardigan. The members were spread over a wide area, often covering many parishes, and it was found convenient to have a number of meeting houses, and several ministers, all equal in status, to care for the scattered congregation. Thus, the Independent church at Llechryd met at Tirllwyd, near the village, and at Rhosygilwen and Castle Maelgwyn, from 1662 onward.

Brynberian chapel was built in 1690 as a branch of the Llechryd church and it came under the care of the ministers of that church, John Thomas of Llwyngrawys and Thomas Beynon.[48] This arrangement continued until 1741 when, on the death of David Sais, Brynberian decided to appoint its own minister in the person of David Lloyd, a member of the church who had assisted as a preacher for the previous nine years. He was ordained on 23 June 1743 and remained in charge until his death in 1764, when he was succeeded by his brother, Thomas Lloyd, who already held the pastorate of Moylegrove. In 1770, Stephen Lloyd, the son of David Lloyd, was ordained minister at Brynberian and, with the expansion of the movement that took place during his ministry, when branches were formed at Felindre Farchog, Maenclochog, Keyston, and Bethesda, near Narberth, it was resolved to appoint Henry George, a church member, to be his co-pastor, and he was ordained in 1790.

The early Independents worshipped in private houses at Newport from the end of the seventeenth century and, by 1726, they did so in 'the house of one Jacob, an old man of deep piety and godliness.' It appears, however, that there was a meeting house at Newport under the care of Thomas Beynon in about 1715. Following the ordination of David Lloyd at Brynberian in 1743, a chapel was built in Lower St Mary Street, and as it was L-shaped, it became known as 'Capel-L'.

In 1817, William Lewis, a student at Carmarthen College, was ordained to be minister at Newport, and to assist Henry George, who had been responsible for Brynberian and all the branch churches since the death of Stephen Lloyd in 1801.

Lewis was instrumental in adding considerably to the numerical strength of the congregation, until his health failed and he died in 1821. In 1822, the church at Newport decided to cease its connection with Brynberian and it appointed Thomas Jones, a student at Llanfyllin College, as its pastor. He took up residence at Betws, where his son, Latimer, was born, who was to become vicar of St Peter's Church, Carmarthen. Owing to a division in his congregation, Jones left for Tiers Cross in 1836 and, in 1843, Samuel Thomas was ordained minister.

In 1844, Capel-L having become too small to house the growing congregation, a substantial chapel to seat 750 worshippers, was built on an adjoining site and named Ebenezer, and the former chapel became the vestry. Ebenezer was erected on land given by William Lloyd of Penfeidr and it was built of stone quarried at Llystyn, by James Salmon, who was later to renovate Newport Castle, at a cost of £794. The chapel has a pediment front of brown dressed stone, with wide eaves and round-headed windows.

Samuel Thomas remained minister until 1861 when J G Morris, a native of Glynarthen, was ordained and he remained minister until he was succeeded in 1911 by Jenkin H Evans, who officiated as minister for the next seven years. His successor, Ben Morris, was a native of Brynberian. He entered Bala-Bangor College in 1896 and was ordained at Carmel Congregational Church, Clydach, in 1899. In 1904 he removed to Pontyberem and, fifteen years later, he came to Ebenezer where he remained until his death in 1942. His powerful eloquence and his 'fire-and-brimstone' sermons distinguished him as one of the last great preachers.

Services and Sunday School were held by the Congregationalists at Blaenmeini farm from 1839 to 1844. when a meeting-house was established at Bwlchyfedwen nearby. A small chapel, known ag Capel y Mynydd, was erected near Parc-y-marriage in 1875 and was in use up to the last war.

The Baptists

The Baptist movement[49] was introduced in north Pembrokeshire by William Jones who, after being imprisoned at Carmarthen for his beliefs, went to the Olchon Valley in Herefordshire and was baptised by immersion by the community of Particular Baptists that had settled there. He returned to west Wales and established a chapel at Rhydwilym in 1668 that gathered members from many parts of the area.

The Baptists are believed to have held preaching services at a private house in Upper Bridge Street in 1675, and from 1760 there was a meeting house to which ministers came from the branch churches that had been established at Cilfowyr, in the parish of Manordeifi, and at Llangloffan. In 1785 the branch at Newport was incorporated into a separate congregation of 87 souls, and, in 1789, the members built Bethlehem Chapel, or 'Capel y Bont' as it was known because of its proximity to the bridge over Afon y Felin. It was rebuilt in 1817, and again in 1855, with seating for 600 persons. It is of dark stucco and stone, and it has tall Gothic windows with delicate interlacing bars.

John Stephens was ordained its first minister in 1795, and he officiated until he emigrated to the United States of America five years later.

Quakers and Others

The Society of Friends, or Quakers, was founded by George Fox, a young Nottingham shoemaker, who began preaching in 1647 and did so with such effect that, by 1656, nearly a thousand of his followers were in jail for refusing to take the oath of abjuration. He came to Pembrokeshire on a preaching campaign in 1657,[50] accompanied by John ap John, the apostle of Quakerism in Wales. Fox stated in his Journal that they visited Tenby, where John ap John was cast into jail 'for standing with his hat on in church, and also Pembroke and Haverfordwest. Quakers were soon holding meetings at Newport, Puncheston, St David's and, possibly, Cilgerran, in north Pembrokeshire. They were persecuted from the outset and, by 1661, several of them had been imprisoned at Haverfordwest, including Lewis David of Llanddewi Velfrey who later purchased land from William Penn and went out to establish the settlements of Haverford and Narberth in Pennsylvania. They held their first Yearly Meeting in Wales at Redstone in 1682.

The emigration to Pennsylvania weakened the Quaker community in Pembrokeshire to such an extent that by 1726 the meetings at Newport were discontinued and it was 'concluded that the Friends of Newport, with as many Friends as have freedom besides, meet once a month at Puncheston, on every second First Day of the month'. There is no name from Newport among the 'sufferers' who were imprisoned at Haverfordwest, and none appears among those who emigrated between 1682 and 1711, the nearest being James Rowland, gentleman, of Rhos y Bayvil, and his brother, John.

According to Evan Jones,[51] two or three families of Plymouth Brethren had settled at Newport. They lived in comfortable circumstances, and were most devout, but caused annoyance by their 'attempts at proselytising and their hatred of our church'.

A unique feature of the neighbourhood is the *Pwnc* festival, consisting of a recital of a chapter from the Bible in chanting tones, followed by a catechising session. The chapter is learnt by heart and the words are intoned in a manner that is reminiscent of a Gregorian chant. As the congregation comprises all ages, there is a difference of pitch, producing parallel lines of music, which the Winchester *Musica Enchiriadis* describes as organum, and which was in vogue until the eleventh century.

Tertullian, writing about 200 AD, refers to Pentecost as the time for hearing a catechism, and the practice appears to have survived in the *Pwnc* festival, which is held at Whitsuntide.

Chapels of the same denomination gather together on Whit Monday to compete against one another. The opening verses are chanted by the whole Sunday school, arrayed on the gallery, while the combined congregations form the audience on the ground floor. The small girls then pipe their words, hastily rushing through the verses allotted to them, followed by the boys, some with their voices breaking, and producing a strident discordance, and with imperfect pauses as they rampage through their verses. The young ladies follow, in melodious but nervous tones, with clipped phrases and obvious relief at reaching the end. while the young men sound more assured and perform with a balanced melody in their voices. The matrons, next, are confident and measure their words, and then their men, middle-aged and steady, chant in perfect unison. Then come the grannies, screeching and breathless, followed by the old men, slow and ponderous as elephants on the march. They all join in for the last few verses with vigour intoning the words until they reach a great crescendo. They stop, instantly and abrupt. The silence is only broken when the catechiser begins his inquisitorial role.

EDUCATION

The 'Report of the Commissioners of Enquiry into the State of Education in Wales', under R R W (later Lord) Lingen, which is commonly referred to as 'The Blue Books', because the three volumes of the report were bound in blue covers, caused a controversy throughout Wales when it appeared in 1847. A public meeting was held at Newport in January 1848, under the auspices of Ebenezer Congregational Church, to consider its findings insofar as religious education was concerned.[1] The meeting repudiated the terms in which the report described Sunday schools and, in particular, the charges made against teachers in such schools, and regretted that, although the Commissioners knew that the number attending the dissenting Sunday schools was three times greater than that which attended those in the Anglican churches, they had come to their conclusions on the evidence of the clergy alone. It was urged that public meetings be held everywhere to expose the false impressions given in the report.

According to the 'Blue Books',[2] Madam Bevan's Central School established at College Square in 1809, was 'practically the parish-school of Newport'. Bridget Bevan was patron of the Circulating Schools founded by Griffith Jones, Llanddowror, and at her death in 1779 she left £10,000 for the continuation of the schools, but her will was contested and the money remained in Chancery during which time it increased threefold in value before it was released in 1804.

The Central School was also a 'model-school for masters', who were sent there for a short period of training before taking up their duties at the Circulating Schools. There were normally two or three masters in training, but there had been as many as thirty attending at the same time. There were 138 pupils in 1811, a number that increased to 160 at its maximum. No registers were kept.

The Master was John Morgan, 'a quiet and inoffensive man' who was 61 years of age at the time of the Report. He had been twice under training, in 1819 at the National Society's Central School at Baldwin's Gardens and, later, for three months 'at The Sanctuary'. He was paid £40 per annum by the trustees, and given a house and garden opposite the school. The Assistant Commissioner, David Lewis, who visited the school, reported that it was held in 'a commodious room', with desks each side and benches squared in the middle, and with a gallery of three tiers at one end. Leaves torn out of *The Tutor's Assistant* were pasted on the walls all round the room. There was no blackboard, and there were no maps, although the master later provided a map of England and Wales and three maps of Palestine. There was no privy and 'the institution was most inadequate as the nucleus of a charity so richly endowed as Mrs Bevan's.'

The 'Rules for Conducting Mrs Bevan's Central Charity School at Newport' set out a code of conduct for the scholars, with suitable punishments. They were 'to be taught spelling and reading with the Catechism and Exposition in the Welsh language, and also to commit to memory and repeat portions of the Scriptures, and selected hymns.'

Then, 'when any shall have made a competent progress in the Welsh language, such scholar shall be placed in an English class to be taught reading, writing and arithmetic.'

John Morgan died in 1865, aged seventy-nine years, after being Master at the school for forty-seven years. He was buried in St Mary's churchyard, and he is commemorated in a memorial window in the chancel of the church.

The Report states that a British School was held in a room above Ebenezer chapel cottage, where a Sunday School was also held. Then there was John Evans's School, kept in 'a wretched cottage, with a bed in the room'. Evans, a former master mariner, was a very old man.

The Central School did not survive long after John Morgan died. Other masters were appointed but, with the implementation of the Education Act of 1870, and the appointment of a School Board, it was closed, despite protests from the church leaders, and the premises were sold and converted into dwelling houses. Building work began on the Board School in Lower St Mary Street the following year and it was opened in 1874, with Joshua R Jones as master. The school was enlarged in 1914 to accommodate two hundred children and it continued to provide education for the children of the parish for the next hundred-and-twenty years, until a new school was opened in Long Street in 1993.

PROMINENT PEOPLE

Most of the sons of Newport who have gained eminence have done so in ecclesiastical and denominational fields. Among the earliest of whom there is record was John Harries,[1] 'the Methodist and Moravian exhorter', who was born at Newport on Good Friday in 1704. He went to reside at St Kennox in the parish of Llawhaden and is referred to as 'John Harries of St Kennox' to distinguish him from the other early Methodist, 'John Harries of Ambleston'. He was most active in south Pembrokeshire and it was he who brought Howel Davies, 'the Apostle of Pembrokeshire' into the county, but he became disillusioned with Methodism in due course and was excommunicated by Howell Harries in 1747. He was credited with having been 'the instrument on the "awakening" of the brothers Relly of Jeffreston',[2] who formed their own sect and, in 1753 he became a member of the Moravian Brethren at Haverfordwest where he was very close to George Gambold, who had married his sister. He died of consumption in 1763 and was buried in St Thomas's churchyard, Haverfordwest, leaving a widow, Margaret, daughter of Llywelyn Davies of Clynfyw, Manordeifi, and a daughter, Ann, who kept school at Haverfordwest.

Sir Watkin Lewes,[3] Lord Mayor of London, was born the youngest son of the Reverend Watkin Lewes, rector of Meline, and his wife, Anne Williams of Ambleston, at Penybenglog in 1740, and he was eighteen years of age, when his father was appointed rector of Newport. He was educated at Shrewsbury and at Magdalene College, Cambridge, where he graduated in 1763, and he was called to the bar three years later. He married Rebecca Eleanor, daughter and coheir of the wealthy Thomas Popkin of Forest, near Swansea, by his wife, Justina Anne, daughter of Sir John Stepney of Llanelli. They had one daughter, who died young.

Lewes was made Sheriff and Alderman of the Lime Street Ward in the city of London in 1772. He was knighted the following year and elected Lord Mayor in 1780. He took an active part in London-Welsh affairs, and was treasurer of the Most Honourable and Loyal Society of Ancient Britons, the first official Welsh Society in London, which established the Welsh Charity School at Ashford, and president of the Honourable Society of Cymmrodorion. He unsuccessfully advocated a British peerage for Lord Milford so that he could succeed him as Member of Parliament for Pembrokeshire, where he had built a mansion for himself at Plas Newydd, St Dogmael's.

Sir Watkin's many parliamentary contests and petitions landed him in pecuniary difficulties and, notwithstanding the sacrifice of his wife's considerable fortune, he was arrested for debt in 1802.[4] He benefited briefly from the death of his elder brother and tried to get a reversal of the decision of the Court of Exchequer that had deprived him of income from his wife's Welsh estates, that was rich in minerals. He spent most of the rest of his life in the London Coffee House on Ludgate Hill, within the rules of the Fleet Prison, and died there, at the age of eighty-one years, on 13 July 1821.

A less well-known native was Captain John Grono,[5] born in Newport in 1763. He appears to have been a member of the Gronow family whose surname lost its final character when he left the area to join the navy. When serving on HMS *Venus* in 1794 he 'received a hurt' and was granted a pension of £5 per annum from the Chatham Chest. In 1798 he emigrated to Australia with his wife, Elizabeth Bristow and two daughters, leaving a son behind in this country, and settled on the banks of the Hawkesbury river in New South Wales. There he established a farm and a ship-building yard on a site that became known as Grono Park. He first made a name for himself as a seal-hunter, catching fur and elephant seals by the tens of thousands.[6]

He is said to have named Thompson Sound after Andrew Thompson, for whom Grono built, and commanded, the schooner *Governor Bligh*. William Bligh, the commander of the *Bounty*, was made Governor of New South Wales in 1805 and he bought land adjacent to Grono's estate. Grono also named Foveaux Strait after Lieutenant-Governor Foveaux, and it is claimed that he gave a sound in the South Island the name Milford Haven, which was later changed to Milford Sound by Lieutenant, later Admiral, John Lort Stokes of Scotchwell, Haverfordwest. Grono Bay, in Doubtful Sound, where he had a sealing station, and Mount Grono, bear his name .

He once rescued ten sealers who had been marooned for four years, from 1809 to 1813, on a remote island and took them to his home, where two of them married two of his seven daughters.

He died in 1847 at the age of eighty-four and was buried near the entrance to Ebenezer Church on the Hawkesbury River of which he was one of the founders.[7] It is tempting to think that he might have been instrumental in naming the church after Ebenezer Chapel at Newport where the family name survived up to the middle of the twentieth century, with Ebenezer Richard Gronow, deacon and precentor.

Joseph Hughes (Carn Ingli)[8] was born at Parciau Mawr on Palm Sunday 1803, the son of David and Hannah Hughes. He received his early education at Mrs Evans's School at Newport, and went on to Mr Philips's School at Haverfordwest in 1816 and then to schools at Carmarthen, Cardigan and Ystrad Meurig before proceeding to St David's College, Lampeter, where he graduated in 1827. He was ordained by the Bishop of St David's in 1828 and became a priest in the following year, when he was given the curacy of Llanfihangel Penbedw. He left Wales in 1830 to become the first incumbent of a new church at Lackwood, Almondbury, near Huddersfield, and later that year, he went as curate at St Jude' Church, Liverpool. In 1836 he returned to Yorkshire and was appointed to the perpetual curacy of Meltham where he remained until he died, in November 1863, and was buried at St Bartholomew's churchyard in Meltham. He wrote *The History of Meltham*, which was regarded as the standard work on that town.

Hughes was one of a number of Welsh clerics who held livings in Yorkshire at that time and was one of the founders of 'The Association of the Welsh Clergy in the West Riding' that was established in 1821. As its first secretary, he made a practice of sending reports of its transactions to newspapers and journals in Wales. His essay, 'English Bishops in Wales' gave an impetus to the movement to have Welsh and Welsh-speaking bishops appointed in Wales.

Hughes retained his contact with Wales, largely through being a keen follower of *eisteddfodau*. He was present at the Gwynedd Society's Eisteddfod at Aberffraw in August 1849 and was admitted a member of the Gorsedd of Bards of the Isle of Britain there, under the bardic name 'Carn Ingli', by the Archdruid Dewi o Ddyfed, a native of Manordeifi who had himself been admitted a member of the Gorsedd by Iolo Morganwg at the Gorsedd ceremony held at the Ivy Bush at Carmarthen in 1819. He was awarded the Cymmrodorion Medal for an essay on *Calondid* (Encouragement) in 1826 and, apart from writing Welsh poems, he translated a number of English ones, including portions of Edward Young's celebrated poem, *The Complaint, or Night Thoughts on Life, Death and Immortality*. In 1858 he assisted Ab Ithel in organising 'The Great Eisteddfod' at Llangollen, where poets wishing to be admitted members of the Gorsedd of Bards had to present themselves for examination by a panel of 'Bards by privilege and custom of the Bards of the Isle of Britain', among whom was Carn Ingli. A prize for a poem to his memory was offered at the Llandudno Eisteddfod in 1864. Owen Hughes,[9] an uncle of Carn Ingli, built a house at Treddafydd in the adjoining parish of Llanychlwydog, where he established a school in which he taught the local children for many years. A stone cross in one of its walls was brought there by him from Mynyddmelyn, where there were said to be a number of such crosses. The building was later converted into a Calvinistic Methodist chapel.

Dr Joshua Hughes,[10] who became Bishop of St Asaph, was born at New Mill on 7 October 1807, the son of Caleb and Margaret Hughes. He was educated at Ystrad Meurig and at St David's College, Lampeter, and was ordained deacon in 1830. He was appointed curate at Aberystwyth in 1831, and then at Carmarthen before becoming the vicar of Abergwili in 1838, and in 1845 he was appointed to the living of Llandovery. He graduated Bachelor of Divinity at Lampeter in 1868 and was made a Doctor of Divinity at Lambeth in 1870. In that year, he was nominated by the Prime Minister, W E Gladstone, to the see of St Asaph. He was the first Welsh-speaking bishop to occupy that see for a hundred-and-fifty years, and did not endear himself to the anglicised element in the diocese by his sustained effort to promote the Welsh language. The close relationship he developed with the Nonconformists, despite the bitter religious controversy of the time, made him popular in other quarters. He died in 1889 and was buried at St Asaph.

He, and his wife, Margaret, daughter of Sir Thomas McKenny, Bart., had two sons and five daughters. One son was Thomas McKenny Hughes, FRS, (1832-1917), professor of Geology at Cambridge, and the other, Dr Joshua Pritchard Hughes, Bishop of Llandaff from 1905 to 1931.

Joshua Hughes had two brothers who also entered holy orders: John Hughes, the vicar of Tregaron, and Jacob Hughes, vicar of Llanrhian. They are both buried in their parents' grave at St Mary's churchyard.

William Morgan,[11] Baptist minister, was born 'early in 1801 near Newport, Pembrokeshire.' He was originally an Independent but when he was working for William Griffiths, the minister of Tabor Baptist Chapel at Dinas, he was converted to the Baptist cause, and he began to preach before he was eighteen years of age. He then went to learn boot-making near Blaenwaun chapel, and when the congregation there realised his ability, they sent him to the school kept by William Owen (Philotheoros) at Cardigan, and from there he went to college at Abergavenny for two years. He was the first Baptist to be ordained in Anglesey, in April 1825, and it was there that he spent the rest of his life. It was said of him that he 'was unequalled except by Christmas Evans' and that he was 'as able as John Elias, but not as lucid'. He wrote a biography of Christmas Evans, to whose widow he devoted the proceeds, but his main work was his *Cysondeb-y-Ffydd* (The Consistency of Faith), a volume of nearly seven hundred pages. He died in 1872.

John Morgan,[12] the son of John Morgan, the headmaster of the Madam Bevan School, was born at Newport in 1827. He was educated at Cardigan Grammar School and at the Anglican Seminary at Abergavenny. He was ordained by Bishop Ollivant of Llandaff in 1850 and, after holding a curacy at Cwmafan, he became vicar of Pontnewynydd in 1852. In 1875 he was appointed rector of Llanilid and Llanharan, and there he remained until his death in 1903. He was a strong protagonist of the Established Church and was regarded by Archbishop Benson of Canterbury as 'the ablest and most erudite of the Church defenders'. He wrote *Four Biographical Sketches* (1892) — of Bishop Ollivant, Bishop Thirlwall, Griffith Jones of Llanddowror and Sir Thomas Phillips (1801-67), and was a contributor to Welsh periodicals and to *The Spectator* and the *Saturday Review*. He translated parts of Anacreon, and of 'Chevy Chase' into Welsh, and some of Williams Pantycelyn's hymns into English. He published a volume of poems entitled *A Trip to Fairyland or Happy Wedlock*, and another called *My Welsh Home: A Poem* (1870)[13] which is written in the metre of Tennyson's 'In Memoriam' and describes his boyhood home at College Square, backing on to the Castle and facing 'the mansions of the gentle race', Berry Hill and Llwyngwair. He died in 1903 and was buried at Llanilid.

David Salmon,[14] principal of the Swansea Training College, was born at Tycanol farm in 1852. His father was James, the son of James Salmon of Llystyn, and his mother was Martha Thomas of Brynberian. The family left Newport in 1855 and settled in the Narberth area. David was educated at Haverfordwest from 1865 to 1869, before proceeding to the Borough Road Normal College in London, where, in 1872, he was appointed to the staff. In 1875 he became the headmaster of the Board School in Belvedere Place, off Borough Road, and in 1892 he was appointed principal of the Swansea Training College for Women, where he remained until his retirement in 1922. In 1919 the University of Wales honoured him with the degree of MA *honoris causa*.

His published work was concerned mainly with aspects of education, and he was a regular contributor to learned journals on matters of historical interest. His essays on 'The Quakers of Pembrokeshire' appeared in the *West Wales Historical Records,* Vols. IX and XII.

He married Mary Wiedhofft of London in 1876 and by her, who died in 1925, he had five children. He and his wife had settled in Pembrokeshire following his retirement. He died in 1944 and was buried at Lampeter Velfrey.

In a personal letter that he wrote in 1939 he recalled that as a schoolboy he used to visit Llystyn and attend services at Ebenezer on Sundays, and 'that once at least I found the sermon dull is proved by my initials, still visible on the Llystyn pew.'

T M Rees, Baptist minister at Holyhead, was born at Brithdir Mawr in 1853 and, when he was fourteen years of age, he was baptised at Caersalem chapel. He entered the Haverfordwest Baptist College in 1870 and was appointed minister at Loughor in 1873. In the following year, he went to America but did not stay there long. For a while he served the chapels of Ffynnonhenri, Cwmduad and Rhydargaeau, but then received a call to return to Loughor. He moved to Gowerton in 1878, where he remained until he was appointed minister of Bethel, Holyhead, in 1891. In 1896, he removed to Barry Docks, but went back to Holyhead three years later to take charge of the Mission to Seamen.

He died in 1904, leaving a widow and nine children, one of whom was Major General Thomas Wynford (Dagger) Rees, CB, CIE, DSO and bar, MC, born at Barry in 1898, who commanded the 19th Indian Division in Burma in the Second World War.

PASTIMES AND RECREATION

George Owen found that 'pastimes and recreation fit for gentlemen' in north Pembrokeshire during the fifteenth century were all to do with the chase.[1] There was no county, he considered, where there was less 'gaming at cards and dice', but bowls and tennis were played, even though they had been forbidden by Henry VIII in 'an Act for mayntenance of artyllerie and debarring of unlawful games' in 1542. The young men practised 'wrastlinge, throwinge the stone, barre and sledge, therein to shew theire actyvities, as also in runneing and leapings.' The pastime that appealed most to him, however, was 'the playe called *Knappan*,'[2] his lively description of which was published by Richard Fenton, in *The Cambrian Register* for the year 1795 as 'An Account of an ancient Game formerly used in Pembrokeshire, South Wales, (and not till of late years entirely disused in some parts of it) from a Manuscript in the Reign of Queen Elizabeth. By one of that Country, who had himself been often an Actor in it.'

The earliest reference to *knappan* occurs in 1557 in the translation of Virgil's *Aeneid* by Thomas Phaer, of Forest, Cilgerran, in which, after stating that 'the Trojan youths played with a whirling ball' he added a note asserting that 'this play is used in Wales and the ball is called *knappan*'. George Owen, being still tied to the traditional belief that the Welsh were descended from 'our first progenitors, the Trojans', seized the opportunity to claim that the game was of equally ancient origin. As it happens, Phaer had made a mistake in translation: the boys played, not with 'a whirling ball' but with 'a whipping top'.

The Romans were said to have had a game of a similar nature, called *harpastum,* and comparisons have been made with ball games played on Shrove Tuesday in Derby and other northern towns, and with 'hurling in the country', a Cornish game described by Richard Carew in 1602.[3]

The only game to which it appears to have borne a relationship was *soule,* that was played in Brittany, though without horsemen, until it was banned in the latter part of the nineteenth century on account of its ferocity and even loss of life.

The game was played with a *cnapan,* whence is derived the anglicized form *knappan,* which was a ball, slightly larger than a cricket ball, made of hardwood, such as box, yew, crab or holly, that had been boiled in tallow so as to make it difficult to hold.

Owen states that the games were playecl 'oftentymes by makeing of match betweene two gentlemen, and at such holidaye or Sondaie as pleased them to appoint the tyme and place.' These were frequently 'the greatest plaies' as the promoting gentlemen would vie with each other to bring the greatest number of players from as many parishes as possible and invite their friends and kinsmen to do likewise. Then there were the settled or standing games that were played on the same five feast days each year. The first was played on Shrove Tuesday on Traeth Mawr between the men of the parishes of Newport and Nevern; the second on Easter Monday at Pontgynon between the men of Meline and Eglwyswrw; the third on the Sunday after Easter at Pwll Du at Llanfihangel Penbedw between the men of that parish and the parish of

Penrydd; the fourth and fifth games at St Meugan's in Llanfair Nantgwyn between the men of Cemais and the men of Emlyn and Ceredigion on Ascension Day and Corpus Christi, on both of which days there was a fair held at nearby Eglwyswrw. The games were attended by victuallers, merchants, mercers and pedlars offering their wares from booths and stalls for the benefit of the large gathering of onlookers.

The players stripped bare, except for a light pair of breeches, so as to save their clothes from being torn into shreds. Early in the afternoon the ball was thrown into the air to start the game and the object was to carry it to an appointed place, such as the church porch. It was hurled and carried backwards and forwards for considerable distances, with no quarter asked or given, and the play often lasted until nightfall. Some of the players were mounted on horseback, armed with 'monstrous cudgells of three foote and a halfe longe' of oak or ash that would knock down an ox, and these were freely used to beat each other and, particularly, those who were on foot, so that they returned home 'with broken heades, black faces, brused bodies, and lame legges, yett laugheinge and merylie jestinge at theire harmes', according to George Owen who claimed that he himself had often taken part 'in this unrulye exercise' and carried its scars on his 'heade, handes and other partes of my bodye'.

The game developed into an occasion for settling old scores and it was abandoned on that account. Fenton stated, in 1811, that in Cemais 'every trace of Cnapan has been worn out for near a century', but it survived in the Teifi valley where the last game was played, between the men of the parishes of Llandysul and Llanwenog, on *Hen Galan* (12 January) 1922. On that date in the following year its place was taken by a Sunday School festival.

Some games, and horse racing in particular, were frowned upon by the religious leaders. Horse races held on Traeth Mawr in 1858 became the subject of great condemnation by the Nonconformist ministers of the locality, and their approaches to the gentry who were the promoters appeared to achieve some temporary success. The races were held again, however, on 13 August 1862 and several participants, on their way from Teifiside, went past Penuel Baptist Chapel, on the Cardigan road, where dedicatory services were being held.[4] The congregation was so large that the service was being conducted in a field opposite the chapel, and the race-goers had to press their way through the worshippers that were, at that moment, coming out of the field after the morning session. At the afternoon service, the Reverend Evan Lewis, Brynberian, prayed that the Creator should indicate his displeasure at such sinful pursuits. At that very moment, it was later affirmed, one of the horses fell as it took a hurdle, and some of the other contestants toppled over it. Several of the riders were injured, and some were said to have been maimed for life. The Reverend Evan Lewis was regarded henceforth as a man possessing considerable divine influence.

A more innocent pastime taking place annually on Traeth Mawr was advertised in a poster issued by the mayor, Thomas Williams of Trellyffaint, giving 'notice of Summer Sports on the Sands on 22 August 1860 at 3.30 p.m.' Entries had to be left at the Llwyngwair Arms by 10 o'clock on the morning of the event. The first race, to be run at 3.30, was an 'Open Race (1 mile)' the prize for which was a saddle and bridle. There then followed at twenty minute intervals, a 'Pony Race (1 mile)', prize a whip and a bridle; a Cob Race, also for 1 mile, for which a saddle was offered as the first prize. At 4.30 p.m. there was an 'Open Foot Race (300 yards)', prize 20s., followed by a 'Foot Race for Boys under 16 years (200 yards)', the winner to receive 10s., and a 'Foot Race for Women (100 yards)' the first prize for which was 'A Guinea Hat', and the second prize 'A Pair of Clogs'. At 5.30 there was to take place the 'Wheelbarrow Race, blindfolded (100 yards) - 1st prize 20s. (Competitors to find their own barrows)'. Then, finally, at 6 o'clock, the 'Donkey Race for a Waistcoat (half a mile)'. The owner of the donkey, presumably, was to receive the waistcoat, for there was for the 'Rider - 2s6d.'

Traeth Mawr was still the venue for the annual Sunday School treats, with tea and children's sports, up to the 1930's. 'Rustic Sports' were also held each August, earlier in the century, in a field near Cromlech House, where there were tennis courts provided. The town had a well established hockey club at one time, and soccer football was played before it was ousted by the oval ball. A nine-hole golf links was laid out adjoining the Warren in 1925.

Ferry boats crossing the river at Parrog charged 1/2d. at low water and 1d. at high tide, although these amounts were increased to 1d. and 2d. respectively before the service ceased. Boating was a favourite pastime, with trips up-river by rowing boat and a cruise in the bay by motor boat. Bathing mainly took place on Traeth Mawr, but the more expert swimmers bathed at Y Cwm and dived off the rock, or off the diving board when that was provided. The Ladies' Bathing Place was a small sandy beach to the west of Y Cwm that was approached by a flight of steps cut in the rock descending from Pen Catman. The nautical highlight of the year, since the latter part of the nineteenth century, was the regatta, with its swimming and diving, rowing and sailing events, held each August. By today, Newport is the most popular sailing and boating centre on the north Pembrokeshire coast.

THE LAST TWO HUNDRED YEARS

During the French Wars poverty strode the Welsh countryside as the people lost their grazing rights, through enclosure, and suffered a scarcity of corn on account of the poor harvests following the wet summers of 1795 and succeeding years. Pembrokeshire also had a direct experience of the revolution when the French *Legion Noire* landed at Carreg Wastad on 22 February 1797. The Newport Division of the Fishguard Fencibles, under its commander, Major William Bowen of Llwyngwair, lost no time in setting out to repel the invader.

The Fencibles had been raised, at his own cost, by William Knox, the son of a Dublin physician and a former Under-Secretary of State for the American Colonies,[1] who had retired to Pembrokeshire in 1782, having purchased the Llanstinan and Slebech estates. His son, Thomas Knox, was placed in command, with a division of two companies under him at Fishguard, and another, of two companies, at Newport under Major Bowen.[2] The strength of the Corps was given as 1 Lieutenant-Colonel, 1 Major, 2 Captains, 4 Lieutenants, 4 Ensigns, 12 Sergeants, 12 Corporals, 8 Drummers, 4 Fifers and 235 rank and file. They wore striped jackets, slouch hats pinned on one side with a leek and had the motto *Ich dien* on their ribbons.[3]

Lieutenant-Colonel Thomas Knox, summoned from a ball at Tregwynt, left for Fishguard Fort and sent a message to Major Bowen to let the Newport Division 'be got under arms and march them to Dinas with what ball cartridge they have', to await there for further orders. 'If I should find it necessary,' he added 'I shall retreat towards Newport.' Bowen must have disregarded the order, for the Newport Division marched 'into the Field in which the Fort is' soon after midnight.

The next morning, Knox, finding that he only had a half of his strength, decided to retreat towards Haverfordwest. At Trefgarn he met Lord Cawdor leading the Castlemartin Troop of the Pembroke Yeomanry Cavalry and, after a brief contretemps, they all marched to Fishguard to face the enemy, who surrendered the next day.

The event was commemorated in poems and ballads,[4] among which were two ballads by Thomas Francis of Fachongle who wrote *Cân am Waredigaeth a gafodd y Brytaniaid o Ddwylaw'r Ffrancod gwaedlyd* (A poem on the deliverance of the Britons from the hands of the bloody French) and *Cân am Wroldeb yr Hen Frytaniaid* (A poem on the bravery of the Ancient Britons).

The acreage returns for 1801[5] show that 143 acres of barley were grown in the parish of Newport that year, and a similar acreage of oats, 22 of wheat, 18 of potatoes and 4 of peas. There were no beans or rye or turnips grown. The rector, David Pugh, in rendering the return to the bishop, begged leave to observe that he was 'confident the scarcity of bread corn in my parish and most others hath not of later years, the year 1799 excepted, been owing so much to a failure of crops as to laying aside the usual tillage and manuring and keeping up such great quantities of grounds for grazing only, by which our farms have required fewer servants and workmen, which I believe has been the chief cause of complaint and of the consequent numerous emigrations of labouring

113

people from this country to America.'[6]

The complaint found expression among the inhabitants of Newport on Friday, 30 January 1801, when a crowd of about a hundred people gathered in Market Street,[7] between one and two o'clock in the afternoon, ready to march to Llwyngwair, led by the Mayor, John Ladd, of Brithdir Bach, bearing a petition to present to George Bowen and his son, James, both of whom were Justices of the Peace. The petition described the suffering of the people, due to the high price of corn. When they arrived at Llwyngwair, however, they found that the gentlemen were not at home, but the mayor entered the house and left the petition to await their return. In it, the people complained that, with their earnings, which amounted to less than 6d a day, they could not afford to buy barley 'now costing 1s 4d (7p) per Cardigan quarter, the oats going to £1 10s (£1.50) 'per teal' and salt at 3d per pound'. They desired peace, but 'the groans of our children for food drove us, in the first instance, to you as our leaders ... We implore you, if at all possible, to reduce the market prices, otherwise we must try our own way of doing so ... God save the King.' On their way back to Newport, the mayor asked John Henton, blacksmith, to halt the marchers so that he could address them. He promised that if they assembled the following market day, and brought their friends with them, he would supply them with barley at 5s (25p) per Winchester, and oats at 2s 4d (12p), out of the storehouses on the Parrog.

The mayor was served with a summons by Thomas Volk, constable, and charged with promoting an unlawful assembly, but he threatened to do 'more mischief yet', for which he was convicted by the magistrate, James Bowen, on 4 February, and was confined for the following three market days. On 15 February, Emanuel Williams and Owen Bowen, two farmers, went bail for him in £20 each, and he was released until he came before the Quarter Sessions the following month. By then, the blacksmith, who was the chief witness, 'had gone to sea'. George Bowen, who had been trained in the law, asked the lord justices to deal leniently with the mayor, despite the seriousness of the charge, and he was allowed to go with a reprimand.

In November 1811, a subscription was opened to alleviate the distress of the poor at Newport by the importation of grain, towards which the Member of Parliament for the county of Pembroke, John Owen of Orielton, contributed £200 to add to the sum of £600 that had already been subscribed. A similar subscription was arranged for the poor of Fishguard.[8]

The impression that Newport had fallen on bad times was plainly given by the early travellers through Wales. Benjamin Malkin,[9] the antiquary, found Newport, in 1803, 'a poor fishing town, partly on the sands, and partly on an eminence, just above the confined bay, with its little port at the mouth of the Nevern ... The market is very small and bad: it was anciently held on the Sunday morning at sunrise; and there was a very great fair on the 16th of June. The town seems to have been of consequence in the time of Edward the First, when there was a large market every Thursday, and the tenants were prohibited from selling any thing without offering it at the market, and paying toll ... It is at present held every Friday.'

Richard Fenton[10] did not have a high opinion of the place in his *Historical Tour through Pembrokeshire*, published in 1811, where he wrote that 'Newport, from its distribution, appears to have had several streets intersecting each other at right angles and dignified with names, giving one on idea of its having, from the first, been a considerable place, probably enlarged when it became a great woollen manufactory three or four centuries after. Though now but a straggling place, meanly built, with many chasms in its streets to fill up, the mere skeleton of the town it once was, yet, at a distance in the aggregate, interspersed with trees as it is, with the ruins of its castle, and a respectable looking church, it has a good effect.'

Fenton's description was paraphrased by Henry Gastineau[11] in his *Wales Illustrated* (1830), which contains his engraving of the ruined castle, with the mill and the miller's house, and the church tower beyond. He commented that 'the harbour is small, and a bar of sand, one mile out, is possible only at high water. It has one fair, July [*recté* June] 27. The market, on Saturdays, has been revived, and the town of late has begun to reassume an increasing trade, and the chasms in its streets are being filled up with buildings.'

Samuel Lewis,[12] in his *Topographical Dictionary of Wales* (1848) states that 'according to [John] Speed, there was anciently a house of Augustine friars at this place, but no particulars of its foundation or history have been preserved.' This is not surprising as the friary was at Newport, Gwent, where it was established some time before 1377.[13] He added that, in Newport, the houses with 'some few exceptions, are indifferently built but, from the intermixture of numerous trees with the buildings, the town has, at a small distance, a pleasingly rural appearance,' and 'the venerable church and the picturesque remains of its ancient castle, render the remote view of it strikingly beautiful'.

None of the houses in the parish of Newport qualified for inclusion in George Owen's list of 'mansion-houses', but Llwyngwair, which stands across the river in the parish of Nevern, regarded Newport as its nearest town and provided employment for a number of its inhabitants as carpenters, builders, coachmen and servants generally.

Houses that are mentioned in the records, and which were of a minor status. include Trecadifor, Holmhouse, Brithdir and Dolrannog. These appear among the many properties that were purchased by George Bowen of Llwyngwair in 1756 from Sir John Pakington, who had inherited the Perrot estate. In 1779 he acquired Berry Hill from Anne Lloyd, widow of Thomas Lloyd of Bronwydd. His son, James Bowen, built Cotham Lodge in 1789 as a dower house, whose widow came to live there after his death in 1816, and it remained in the family until it was sold in the aftermath of the Great War.

The end of the Crimean War, brought about by the Treaty of Paris, was celebrated at Newport with an invitation from the Mayor, the Reverend Llewelyn Thomas, the Aldermen and Burgesses, to meet 'Thomas Davies Lloyd, Esquire, Lord of the Barony of Kemes' and 'to partake of a Cold Collation within the precincts of the ancient Castle of Newport' on 29 May 1856, 'in celebration of the happy restoration of

Peace and Harmony among the nations of Europe.' Tickets were 'issued at the Llwyngwair Arms at 1 p.m. precisely.' A procession was formed 'to meet the Lord of the Barony entering the boundary of the Corporation at 12 noon.' The 'cold collation' was served 'within the precincts' as Lloyd had not yet commenced to build a residence there.

The tithe war, which raged throughout west Wales in the latter part of the nineteenth century, was felt more in the surrounding parishes than in Newport itself. The tithe, which had been the method of financing the church since biblical times, became the cause of a sense of grievance in a largely Nonconformist community. Since 1836 the payment of one-tenth of one's farm produce in kind had been converted into a monetary tithe charge. Nonconformists who never entered a church and had little, or no, contact with the parish priest, were disinclined to pay the tithe charge, and there was a general demand that the Church of England be disestablished in Wales, as it had been in Ireland.

Rural discontent was further accentuated by the onset of an agricultural depression with the rapid fall in the price of grain and other farm products. In 1886, requests were made to the clergy to reduce the tithes by ten per cent, and when this was refused, payment was withheld. This affected the financial position of the clergy and notices of distraint were issued. The first auction of distrained goods in the neighbourhood was held at Moylegrove in August 1887. A large gathering of objectors attracted a heavy presence of police who, together with the efforts of a Nonconfirmist minister, managed to keep the peace, apart from the throwing of rotten eggs, and the distrained goods were bought back by, or for, the owner. The agents employed by the Ecclesiastical Commissioners to recover the tithes were often met by hostile crowds, blowing 'tithe-horns' and beating tin vessels and throwing missiles to such an extent that they often had to abandon their visits, despite, having a police escort. The Tithe Rent Charge Recovery and Redemption Act of 1891 made landlords alone responsible for the payment of tithes, and the money was recoverable in the county courts, instead of by the tithe agents.

Friendly Societies were established in the eighteenth century for the purpose of providing their members with financial benefit during sickness or infirmity, and their promotion was encouraged by the magistrates so as to keep people off the poor rates. The Wrexham Neighbourly Society was the first to be founded in Wales, in 1744, but the earliest to be recorded in Pembrokeshire was the True Briton Society established in the parish of Llanfihangel Penbedw in 1772, which met at Tafarn Boncath each month with members contributing 6d (two and half pence) for the fund and 2d for beer. Some societies formed themselves into Orders, the first of which in Wales was the Ancient Order of Foresters, the Carningli Lodge of which was formed at Newport in 1877, holding its meetings at the Commercial Hotel every month. Its members paraded wearing green sashes with the emblems of the Order, and carrying ceremonial bows and arrows. The Loyal Kemes Lodge of Oddfellows, which had been founded in 1840, met at the Llwyngwair Arms Hotel. Each lodge had up to 150 members.

The only order indigenous to Wales was the Philanthropic Order of the True Ivorites,[14] named after Ifor Hael, the fourteenth century patron of

Dafydd ap Gwilym. It was founded at Wrexham in 1836, but its headquarters moved to Carmarthen two years later, and the Ivorites added to the usual aims of a friendly society, the promotion of the Welsh language. The fellowship and the brotherhood of the Ivorities 'Club' that met at Tafarn Bwlch in about 1780 was the subject of a poem written by the poet Ioan Siencyn.

Some of the societies had their ritual, with passwords and secret signs. The Calvinistic Methodists, in 1840, forbade its members from belonging to the Oddfellows on this account. The Ivorities and the Calvinistic Methodists agreed, however, in disapproving illegal practices and the latter, at its association meeting held at Newport in 1843, condemned 'the lawless and anarchical spirit' of Rebecca and published a notice urging their congregation to expel those who participated in its demonstration or who even sympathised with the movement.[15] Newport was not affected by the Rebecca riots except that, in 1843, it had a small detachment of Royal Marines stationed in the town as part of the defence of Pembrokeshire.[16]

The town was provided with facilities for banking by 1880 when the National Provincial Bank of England opened a sub-office on Fridays and fair days, with Reuben R Storey as manager. Lloyd's Bank opened an agency, under the Cardigan branch, at Newport in 1891.[18] The agent was Thomas Jenkins, who became a familiar figure in the town, and the agency became known as 'Banc Twm Siencyn' and was the subject of some topical verses. When the Parish Council was established in 1894, he was appointed its first clerk, and he also acted as rate collector. going from house to house on horseback. He was succeeded by T Y Lewis, who was to become the manager of the Haverfordwest branch. His position, as clerk-in-charge, was upgraded when he was followed by David Davies, who was appointed manager in 1928. The London City and Midland Bank had opened a branch before 1916, with W W Rees as manager, and Barclay's Bank had an office at Maescynon, in Market Street.

The Newport Parish Council was formed in 1894 with the Rev J G Morris, pastor of Ebenezer, as its first chairman, and Thomas Jenkins, of Lloyd's Bank, was appointed Clerk.

New telegraphic instruments were installed at the Post Office in 1905 and it was reported in the *County Echo*[18] on 15 February 1906 that the clerks had become very proficient with the Morse 'sounder'. Miss Phillips, 'the obliging assistant to Mrs Lamb', the post mistress, had despatched a message of two hundred words in an incredibly short space of time 'and without any stoppages', and the whole had appeared in a London newspaper the following day.

In the same year, the inhabitants of Newport had gazed with wonder, and a little trepidation, at the sight of a motor lorry belonging to Messrs Rees Brown of Haverfordwest.[19] Children had collected in groups to look at 'the wonderful mechanism', while their elders stood in surprise in their doorways. The editor of the *County Echo* opined that 'the day of the horse waggon is in danger of passing into the limbo of the past'. He also reported that Bishop Owen of St David's had ordered a motor car and anticipated that he would use it to visit outlying churches for confirmation services. He warned the people who were accustomed to seeing his lordship in his top hat that they would have to become accustomed to recognising him wearing a motoring cap, for it would need 'a firm clutch with both hands to keep a top hat of the size of the Bishop's in the perpendicular during a motor ride on this stormy coast.'

At the banquet following his installation as mayor in November 1920,[20] Councillor J O Vaughan, who represented Newport both on the County and District Councils, said that he looked forward to the time when the town would have electric lighting, a public water supply and a proper sanitary system. He had already got the County Council's Highways Committee to agree to have the main roads tar-sprayed. which had done much towards keeping down the dust from passing vehicles. Alderman (later Sir) George Bowen expressed his appreciation of the coach service that had been provided between Cardigan and Fishguard Railway Station by the Great Western Railway at the request of the War Agricultural Executive Committee. A service was also provided by D. Howard Roberts, a local businessman, who established Pioneer Motors.

The retiring mayor, Dr David Havard, was congratulated for having established 'Our Boys' Fund for returning ex-servicemen, and for inaugurating an annual eisteddfod, which had raised funds towards building a Memorial Hall, the site for which had been given by his mother, the ex-Mayoress.

Councillor Vaughan lost no time in calling a public meeting at which it was decided to build a hall of corrugated iron with a stone frontage at an estimated cost of £2,000, the plan for which had been drawn up, without charge, by the district surveyor, Dewi Evans.[21] Captain Tom Evans, Cambria, whose hair had gone white overnight, it was said, as he sailed through the Straits of Magellan, did not consider that such a building

Opening of the Memorial Hall, 1922.

would be a worthy memorial to the fallen and proposed that the hall should be built of traditional materials, and this was agreed. His wife, and the ladies of Newport, raised funds in order to add a Library and Reading Room where 'the young people of the town could spend their leisure hours, instead of going to public houses.' The Reading Room was opened by Alderman Vaughan in March 1923, while the hall itself was offically opened in September of that year by the Mayor, Frederick Edward Withington of Bicester, who was a son-in-law of Sir Marteine and Lady Lloyd.[22]

A field gun that had been in use during the Great War, was presented to the town and placed in front of the hall. It was popularly known as 'The Cannon' and it served as an outsize toy for boys to climb over, and to mount the barrel until it shone. It must have lost its appeal to later generations, for it became a rusty hulk and was carted away to end its days ingloriously on a rubbish dump on The Marsh. A gun barrel from an earlier war, reputedly the Crimean, which the Goverment distributed to towns in various parts of Britain in 1857, was built into the corner of a garden wall at the foot of Feidr Brenin.[23]

While preparing the foundations for the Memorial Hall, in January 1921, the bases of two fifteenth century pottery kilns that were revealed proved to be those of the only medieval Welsh pottery kiln yet discovered.[24] The base diameter of each kiln was 5ft 8 ins, and round each of them there ran a flue, two and a half feet wide, connecting with the arch of the fire-hole. Each kiln had a clay platform laid on slate slabs, with vents round the circumference. The drums were also built of slate slabs, presumably obtained from the cliff-quarries. A plan of the kilns and a section of one was made by Professor (later Sir) Mortimer Wheeler, who visited the site. A wide range of ware was found, including floor and ridge tiles, pitchers and cooking pots, with the characteristic yellowish-green glaze of the period. One of the kilns has been preserved beneath the hall stage.

An earthware jug and a two-handled pot found when clearing the undercroft at the castle, were evidently made in the kilns. Together with some ware fragments, they were deposited in the Carmarthen Museum.

The excavation of the burgage plots in Long Street, in 1991-2, produced seven thousand sherds of pottery, most of it of medieval date and made in the local pottery kilns.

The town obtained its water supply, before it was piped in the 1930's, from wells, some of which had been fitted with a piece of pipe, or guttering, to form a *pistyll*, or spout. The inhabitants would have to fetch their drinking water in a water-can, and elderly ladies, and the more genteel who did not have their own maids, would pay boys who were strong enough to carry the cans a few pence a time. The main sources of supply were:

Pistyll y Cotham, set in an arched recess built by the owners of Cotham Lodge at the bottom of Slade Lane, from which the inhabitants of the western part of the town obtained their water. *Pistyll y Cnwce*, gushing out of the hedgerow beyond the site of the gallows tump, on the side of the main road. *Pistyll y Felin*, below Pont Henrietta Mair, (named after the wife of Sir Thomas Davies Lloyd), which served the inhabitants of the middle of the town. *Pistyll Dandre,* adjoining the garden of Dandre Cottage. *Pistyll y Cei,* issuing out of a wall at the end of the Quay Wall, by Craig-y-môr. *Pistyll Dewi,* in a field behind Llys Dewi and near the site of Capel Dewi. *Pistyll Samson,* at Penybont, near the earthwork, Bedd Samson. *Pistyll Carn Ffoi,* off the Bedd Morus road, near Treffynnon.

Where the water was obtained direct from the well, it was raised with a saucepan, or similar utensil, and poured into the water can or, less hygienically, the can was dipped into the well. The well was emptied and cleaned at regular intervals, and the water was always crystal clear, even when the well lay alongside a roadway.

Ffynnon Gurig is a short way upstream of Newport Bridge, with a fragment of its masonry remaining, and near to it was the site of St Curig's chapel. *Ffynnon Drieg* lies by the roadside at Nantyblodau and was held to be a curative well. *Ffynnon Cippinstone* was also a roadside well in Feidr Ganol, that was demolished for the purpose of road widening. *Ffynnon Garn Cwn* (SN 063384) is commonly known as the Wishing Well. It cures warts and, by dropping a pin in the well, one's dearest wish will be fulfilled, provided it is kept a secret. Like many coastal wells, it is believed to be tidal. At the junction of Upper St Mary Street and East Street was *Y Pwmp,* a pump that served the eastern part of the town.

A sanitary system was installed in the mid-thirties in the face of intense opposition to a sea outfall, which later had to be extended out to sea. Street lighting by oil lamps had been introduced in 1883, when the facilities on the Parrog were also improved by the provision of roads and steps. The provision of an electricity supply, for public and domestic lighting, took place in the early twenties, generated in the first instance by Messrs Williams and Evans at the Central Garage.

Although early travellers in Pembrokeshire despaired of the state of the towns and villages, they found the countryside 'excelling in its scenery' and, in addition to this discovery, the beneficial effect of sea-bathing had been realized.[25] Tenby had become a resort for bathing by 1760 and, in 1782 St Julian's, the fishermen's chapel, was converted into a 'bathing-house' for his patients, to whom he prescribed seawater bathing, by Dr John Jones, 'an intelligent apothecary from Haverfordwest', whose daughter was married to Thomas Lloyd of Bronwydd, lord of Cemais.

Newport became a holiday resort half-way through the nineteenth century, and its popularity grew after the coming of the railway to Clarbeston Road. The Reverend Evan Jones was able to state, in 1890, that 'an important part of the town of Newport is what may be called the sea-bathing suburb of Parrog' where there were the 'pretty lodging houses, which so many visitors from all parts of England and Wales make their temporary homes during the sea-bathing season of summer'. He was of the opinion that 'a larger number of lodging houses' was required and hoped that 'some enterprising capitalists' would soon supply the need, or that 'a limited liability company be formed for securing such a desirable end'.

An indication of the holiday accommodation available on the Parrog in 1916 may be gathered from the advertisements that appeared in the first guide-book to Newport published that year 'under the authority and direction of the Mayor [Sir Evan D Jones, Bart.] and Corporation':[27]

Holidaymakers arrive at The Angel.

Property	Bedrooms available	Proprietor
Wellfield Grove	5	Mrs J Richards
Craig-y-môr	4	Mrs Ida Lewis
Glan-y-môr	6	Mrs C Michael
Seagull Cottage	3	E John
Rock House	5	Mrs M Adams
Bryn-y-môr	7	J Ellis
Swn-y-don	6	Mrs Samuel
Bettws	6	E A Evans

There were some other houses offering accommodation on or near the Parrog making some 50-60 beds available in all.

In the town, three hotels advertised holiday accommodation but none specified the number of bedrooms. The Llwyngwair Arms Hotel, proprietor Thomas Lewis, offered a 'Motor Car for hire'; the Commercial Hotel (D Thomas) had a garage and cars for hire, one of which carried twelve persons, and also boasted 'the only billiards table at Newport', and the Angel Temperance Hotel, owned by James Thomas, baker and confectioner, offered 'well-aired beds'. Two private houses also offered accommodation: Myrtle Cottage (Mrs M Jones), two bedrooms, and Welford House (Miss B Evans), formerly the Plough Inn, three bedrooms. The houses along the sea-front were largely occupied by people from the professional classes who brought their families, year after year. Farming families and country people from the immediate hinterland came bringing their own food supplies with them, and Newport was also

Houses on the Parrog.

a popular resort for miners and others connected with the coal-mining industry who came for their annual holidays until the Great Strike had its full effect in the early thirties.

Since 1952 Newport has occupied a prominent place in the Pembrokeshire Coast National Park, which was designated that year.[28]

The Swan family.

The Coast Path, after following the coast from St Dogmael's, enters the parish at Newport Bridge and proceeds along the Marsh to the Parrog and on to Y Cwm and over the cliffs to Aber Rhigian and Aber Forest.

As the coast is the main attraction in the National Park, there is a heavy concentration of people in a relatively small area during the summer season. The increase in the number of holiday homes, particularly on the Parrog, which are occupied for only short periods and remain empty for the rest of the year, also imperils the quality of life of the local community. For these, and other reasons, every effort has to be made to protect the natural environment, its beauty and its amenities. Failure to do so will place at risk the very things we all enjoy.

Place Names

Aber Forest	*aber* (estuary) + Forest (name of farm but referring to former Rhigian forest described as *bosci de Riwgian* in 1394.
Aber Rhigian	*aber* (estuary) + *Rhigian* (q.v.)
Aber Ysgol	aber (estuary) + *ysgol* (ladder).
Afon Clydach	*afon* (river) + Clydach (q.v.)
Afon y Felin	'the mill brook': formerly called Nant Mawr.
Afon Ysgolheigion	'the scholars' brook': it flowed past the school built in 1871: formerly called Gilles Lake (q.v.).
Alltclydach	*allt* (wood) + Clydach (q.v.).
Bedyddfan	*baptistry* built for Bethlehem Baptist Chapel in 1855 to baptize by immersion in water diverted from Afon y Felin.
Bedd Morus	*bedd* (grave) of Morus who was a highway robber or, perhaps, a thwarted lover.
Bedd Samson	*bedd* (grave) of Samson, a mythical giant.
Benet, Y	place where the bent-grass grows, in this case marram grass.
Berry Hill	*beorg* (hill) + hill: also called The Bury.
Betws	OE *bede hus* (bede house, house of prayer, chapel of ease).
Blaenffynnon	*blaen* (source) + *ffynnon* (well).
Blaenpant	*blaen* (end) + *pant* (hollow, valley).
Blaenwaun	*blaen* ((end) + *gwaun* (moorland, heath).
Brithdir	*brith* (speckled) + *tir* (land).
Brodan	*brwd* (boiling, fierce) + *an* (dimunitive suffix).
Burrows, The	another name for The Warren (q.v.).
Bury, The	see Berry Hill.
Capel Curig	St Curig's chapel, near Newport Bridge.
Capel Dewi	St David's chapel.
Carn Cŵn	*carn* (cairn) + *cŵn* (dogs)
Carn Ffoi	*carn* (ca;rn) + *ffoi* (retreat)?
Carn Ingli	*carn* (cairn) + *Ingli* whom George Owen (1603) stated was a giant.
Carn Lwyd	*carn* (cairn) + *llwyd* (grey).
Carreg Goetan	*carreg* (stone) + *coetan* (quoit), also referred to as Carreg Coetan Arthur. Arthur's Quoit was a common name for a burial chamber.
Cat Rock	see *Y Gath*.
Cerrig	*cerrig* (stones).
Clydach	a common name for a river in south-west Wales derived from the Irish *cledagh*, a quick flowing river with a stony bed.
Cnwc-y-grogwydd	*cnwc* (hillock, tump, from the Irish *cnocc*) + *crogwydd* (gallows): the site of the manorial gallows, also called Warrentree.
Cwm Dewi	*cwm* (combe) + *Dewi* (David), running down from Capel Dewi.

Dandre	*dan* (under, below) + *tref* (town).
Dolrannog	Dr B G Charles traces to *Talleronnauc* (c 1250) and maintains it is derived from *tal* (end, front) + *yr onnog* (place where ash-trees grow).
Dŵr-y-felin	*dŵr* (water) + *y felin* (of the mill).
Feidr Brenin	*meidr* (lane) + *brenin* (king).
Feidr Facholyn	Dr B G Charles suggests *Feidr Farchoglyn* as in *Ffordd Fachoglyn* in Bayvil parish: *meidr* (lane) + *marchog* (knight) + *llyn* (pond, lake).
Feidr Felin	*meidr* (lane) + *melin* (mill).
Feidr Gerigog	*meidr* (lane) + *cerigog* (stony).
Ffynhonnau	*ffynhonnau* (wells).
Ffynnon Bedr	*ffynnon* (well) + *Pedr* (Peter).
Ffynnon Drieg	*ffynnon* (well) + *triagl* (treacle, balm).
Fronhaul	*bron* (breast, slope) + *haul* (sun).
Gilles Lake	*Gilles* (personal name) + *lake* (stream).
Gwachal Sythu	*gochel* (avoid) + *sythu* (freezing).
Gweunydd	*gweunydd* (low-lying marshy ground).
Holmhouse	*holms* (water-meadows).
Keeping Stone	the earliest form is *Gyby stone* (1749).
Llannerch-y-bleiddiau	*llannerch* (glade, clearing) + *y bleiddiau* (of the wolves).
Llwyngwair	*llwyn* (tree, grove) + *Gwair* (personal name) or *gwair* (bend, curve): cf. Llwyngwair is situate in a bend of the river Nevern.
Nant Mawr	*nant* (valley, stream) + *mawr* (great, big): an early name for Afon y Felin.
Nant-y-blodau	*nant* (valley, stream) + *y blodau* (flowers).
Nevern	the name first appears as *Neuer* c 1200 and later as *Nyfer*, or *Nant Nyfer*, 'the valley through which the Nyfer flows'. The meaning is not known.
Newport	*Novus burgus* 'new town' appears as *Nuport* in 1282 and *Newburgh* in 1296, and settled as *Newport* where *port* means 'town'.
Pant-yr-hydd	*pant* (hollow, valley) + *yr hydd* (of the hart).
Pant-y-rhedyn	*pant* (hollow, valley) + *y rhedyn* (of the ferns).
Parciau	*parciau* (fields).
Parc-y-marriage	appears c 1275 as *Makmareis* which Dr B G Charles gives as OE *mearc* (boundary mark) + *mareis* (a marsh).
Parc-y-person	*parc* (field) + *person* (parson).
Parrog	OE *pearroc* (enclosure, paddock), used here to mean 'flat land along the shore'.
Penbrenkis	*pen* (top) + *bryncws* (brink, verge). ?
Pen Catman	*pen* (headland) + Cadman (personal name).
Penffald	*pen* (hill-top) + *ffald* (pound, pinfold).
Pengawse	*pen* (end) + *cawsai* (causeway).
Penllain	*pen* (top, end) + *llain* (strip of land.
Penrhiw	*pen* (top) + *rhiw* (hill).

Pen-y-bont	*pen* (end) + *y bont* (of the bridge)
Pig-y-benet	*pig* (point) + *y benet* (of the land where the bent-grass, or marram, grows).
Pont-heb-wybod	*pont* (bridge) + *heb wybod* (without knowing, i.e. concealed).
Pont Henrietta Mair	a stone pillar on the bridge commemorates Henrietta Mary, wife of Sir Thomas Davies Lloyd, who died in 1871. The inscription *Y gwir yn erbyn y byd* (The truth against the world) is the motto of the Gorsedd of Bards.
Prendergast	is believed to be the name of a Fleming who settled at Haverfordwest: Maurice de Prendergast was among the Pembrokeshire knights who landed in Ireland in 1169.
Rhigian	*rhiw* (hill, slope) + Cian (personal name) ?
Rhosnanty	*rhos* (moor, heath) + *nentydd* (brooks).
Shiphill	sheep + hill.
Slade	slade (valley).
Tafarn-sbeit	*tafarn* (tavern) + *sbeit* (in spite of), according to Dr B G Charles.
Trecadifor	*tref* (homestead) + Cadifor (personal name).
Trewreiddig	*tref* (hamestead) + Moreiddig (personal name).
Warren, The	*warren*, land in which rabbits abounded or were preserved.
Warrentree Lake	*warrentree* (gallows) + *lake* (stream).
Waunoerfa	*gwaun* (moorland, heath) + *oerfa* (cold place).
Y Cei	*y* (the) + *cei* (quay).
Y Gath	*y* (the) + *cath* (cat) or *?garth* (enclosure).
Y Gelli	*y* (the) + *celli* (grove, copse).
Y Gribyn	*y* (the) + *cribyn* (ridge, top).

NOTES

BEFORE NEWPORT

1   Vincent 313
2   Leland 113
3   Camden 758
4   Morris 1878 408
5   Owen, George ii 1897 439-41
6   Charles 1992 149,161
7   Morris 1748 Plan 19
8   Charles 1992 165
9   *ibid* 148
10   Ellis-Gruffydd 1 26-7
11   John 23
12   *ibid* 31-2
13   Bassett 264
14   Ellis-Gruffydd 2 27
15   *Arch Camb* 1922 494-6
16   Dyfed Archaeological Trust Report 1991-92
17   Rees 15-6
18   Owen, George. 1994, 196
19   Wyndham 93
20   Rees 16-7
21   Fenton 1811 554
22   Wade-Evans 11
23   Owen, Geo. 1994 108
24   Jones and Jones 85
25   Nash Williams 200
26   Owen, Geo. ii 1897 509
27   *ibid* i 1892 143 n.
28   Jones, E 1890 10
29   Jones, F 1954 4, 208
30   Charles 1992 50
31   Gruffydd R G 198-209
32   *Baronia de Kemeys* 48

NEWPORT CASTLE

1   King 1983 395
2   Lloyd, J E 584, 617
3   Turvey 64, 66
4   Hogg, 107, 117
5   Browne *et al* 6
6   King and Perks 1949
7   Browne *et al* 31
8   *Brut y Tywysogynon* s.a. 1215
9   Lloyd, J E 721
10 King 1981 12
11 *Baronia de Kemeys* 21
12 King and Perks 1949
13 Griffiths 116
14 *Baronia de Kemeys* 99
15 *ibid* 95
16 *Arch Camb* 1904 275
17 Charles, 1973 86
18 Bronwydd 1068
19 Jones, F. 1984, 339
20 *Arch Camb* 1859 335
21 *Arch Camb* 1904 276
22 Browne *et al* 28-9
23 *Inventory* 275
24 *Carmarthen Journal* 1 November 1867
25 Browne *et al* 28-9
26 *Baronia de Kemeys* 14-24
27 Browne *et al* 14-24
28 Lloyd, T. 53

THE LORDS OF CEMAIS

1   Lyte 2
2   King 1981 8
3   Davies, R R 86
4   Lloyd, J E 567n
5   Turvey 57
6   *ibid* 63
7   Lloyd, J E 431
8   Radford 7-8
9   Lyte 12
10   Davies, R R 52-4
11   Turvey 63
12   *ibid* 61
13   Davies, R R 222
14   Gerald of Wales 170-1
15   Lloyd J E 578
16   Turvey 64-6
17   King 1983 395, 402
18   Lyte 16
19   Charles 1973 164
20   I'Anson 12
21   Griffiths 94
22   Lyte 21-2
23   Owen, H. 1918   III 6
24   Round 1930 78
25   McKisack 10
26   *ibid* 22
27   Griffiths 24,98
28   Beaumont 3-4
29   Lyte 24-5
30   Griffiths 116
31   Owen, H 1918 III, 32-3
32   Griffiths 115
33   ibid 137-8
34   Mackie 141-3
35   Bronwydd 7018
36   *ibid* 1408
37   *ibid* 1198
38   *ibid* 1182
39   Owen, George. 1994, 1867, 223-4
40   Charles 1973 7-8
41   Bronwydd 1100
42   Owen, George ii 1897 524
43   Owen, George 1994 xv-lxi
44   Charles 1973 29
45   *ibid* 55
46   Morgan, P B 377-405
47   Lloyd, T. 53

THE BOROUGH

1   Soulsby 199
2   *Baronia de Kemeys* 50-1
3   Charles 1973 163
4   Lyte 16
5   Lloyd, J E 721
6   Lyte 17
7   Owen, H 1914 II 5
8   Lyte 17-8
9   *Baronia de Kemeys* 49
10   Charles, 1973 165
11   Powicke 433
12   *Baronia de Kemeys* 67-8
13   ibid 77-8
14   Soulsby 200
15   Charles 1951 120-7
16   *Baronia de Kemeys* 10
17   Dyfed Archaeological Trust Report 1991-92
18   Charles 1951 127-135
19   Howells, B E & K A 14
20   *Arch Camb* 1904 276
21   Charles, 1951 130
22   I 1904 277
23   Howells, B E & K A 16-7
24   ibid 15
25   Bronwydd 1257
26   ibid 1257

FAIRS AND MARKETS

1   Owen, Geo. 1994 144, 276
2   *Almanc y Cymro* 1883 17
3   Charles 1951 39
4   *Bulletin of the Board of Celtic Studies* iii, 315
5   Bronwydd 6783
6   *ibid* 6691
7   Charles 1951 135
8   *Baronia, de Kemeys* 57-60
9   Owen, George, 1994 143, 27S-6
10   *Baronia de Kemeys* 57
11   Fenton 1811 553
12   Charles 1967 126
13   Howells, B E & K A 14
14   Bronwydd 1009
15   Jones, F 1979   55

THE MAYOR

1   *Baronia de Kemeys* 50
2   See p.88 above
3   Charles 1951 138
4   *Report of Municipal Corporation Commissioners* 1835 354
5   Charles 1951 39
6   Charles 1973 19
7   *ibid* 91
8   *Baronia de Kemeys* 1-42
9   Owen, Geo iii 1906 131
10   Charles 1973 95-8
11   Jones, F 1979 38
12   *ibid* 39
13   Bronwydd 3336
14   *ibid*   6635
15   *ibid*   4418-9
16   *ibid*   7025
17   *ibid*   3410
18   *ibid*   3232-40
19   *County Echo* 16 November 1899
20   *ibid* 4 January 1906
21   *ibid* 15 November 1906
22   *ibid* 1 November 1900
23   Evans, E J 166-7

LAW AND ORDER

1   *Baronia de Kemeys* 22-3
2   Charles 1951 40
3   Owen, George. ii 1897,   451
4   *ibid* 454-60
5   Charles lg51 128
6   *ibid* 38-40
7   *ibid* 43-5
8   Charles 1973 73-4
9   Miles 1976 22
10   Jones, F 1979 41
11   Miles 1976 27
12   Bronwydd 3955
13   Thorne 1994 235
14   *Report of Municipal Corporation Commissioners, 1835* 354
15   Thorne 1994 247, 249
16   *Law Commission Report,* 1976 8
17   Bronwydd 6776-6780
18   Lloyd, K H 14

THE PORT OF NEWPORT

1   Tucker 1958 7
2   Owen, Geo. 1994 46
3   Lewis, E A 311
4   *ibid* 315
5   *ibid* viii-ix
6   *ibid* 83-4
7   *ibid* xxxiv
8   Owen Geo. 1994 59-60
9   *ibid* 149
10   Lloyd, E J 67-8
11   Morris 1748 13
12   Owen, Geo 1994 83
13   Lewis, S 268
14   Owen, Geo. 1994   82
15   *ibid* 60, 123-4, 139-40, 269
16   *ibid* 124, 139, 269
17   Lewis, S 268
18   Howells, B E & K A 11
19   Jenkins, J G 1974 239, 322
20   *ibid* 152
21   Charles 1951 40
22   Jones, F 1984 337
23   Owen, G D 101
24   Lewis, E A 83
25   *ibid* 99
26   Lloyd, H A 15
27   Richards, Ll 1958   15
28   Owen, Geo. 1994 72
29   Davies, W 1815
30   Jones, F. 1979   47
31   Morris, L. 12-3
32   Bronwydd 294
33   Howell, J. 359
34   *ibid* 214
35   Lloyd, D & M 112-4
36   Bronwydd 6674-6689
37   Jenkins, J G 1982 84
38   *Cymru a'r Mor/Maritime Wales* 11 (1987) 19
39   Jenkins, J. G. 1982 85
40   *ibid* 122-3
41   Davies, D. 1-22
42   Thomas, P. 19-22 86 *passim*
43   Jenkins J G 1982 172-235
44   *County Echo* 5 June - 30 October 1958
45   Bennett, T 61-2
46   Goddard, T 45-6
47   *Newport, Pembrokeshire: The Official Guide* 1916 14
48   Howell, D W 28

ROADS AND TRANSPORT

1   Jones, E. 1890 63
2   Ballinger 37
3   Jones, E. 1890 63
4   Bronwydd 3962-5
5   Slater's Directory 1858
6   Ballinger 36
7   Owen, Geo. 1906 *folio* 40
8   Fenton 1811 553
9   Minutes of the Penbont
     Bridge Committee 1891-4

CHURCH AND CHAPELS

1   Wade-Evans 11
2   Owen, Geo ii 1897 509
3   Owen, Geo 1994 144, 276
4   Stephens, M. 104
5   Fenton 1811 131
6   Owen Geo i 1892 143 n
7   Jones, T T 221
8   Gregory 14
9   Jones, E. 1890 65
10 Lewis, S. 268
11 Wallace-Hadrill 16
12 Fenton 1811 546
13 Nash-Williams 200
14 *Baronia de Kemeys* 51,57
15 Green and Barker 223-24
16 Howells, B E & K A 11
17 *ibid* 11
18 Jones, E 1890 22
19 *ibid* 79
20 Green and Barker 223-4
21 Charles 1973 29
22 Green and Barker 223-4
23 *Dictionary of Welsh Biography* 891
24 *ibid* 811
25 Williams, A H 87
26 Jones, E. 1890 20
27 *Arch Camb* 1859 334-5
28 Jones, E. 1894 61
29 Baker 136
30 *Inventory* li
31 Evans, J T 71
32 Wallace-Hadrill 23
33 *County Echo* 21 September 1921
34 Jones, E 1890 23-4
35 Charles 1947 56-7
36 *ibid* 63
37 Saunders, E. 33
38 Roberts I 171, 210
39 *ibid* 149
40 *ibid* 211
41 *ibid* 163
42 *ibid* II 163
43 Williams, A H 87
44 *ibid* 94
45 *ibid* 97-8
46 *ibid* 100-25
47 Rees and Thomas, J. 86-7
48 *ibid* 38-43
49 Jones, D. 222-4
50 Salmon, D 1-32
51 Jones, E. 1894 66

PROMINENT NATIVES

1   *Dictionary of Welsh Biography* 341
2   Phillips 572-6
3   *Dictionary of Welsh Biography* 543
4   Thorne (ed.) 431
5   McNab 85 passim
6   Grono-Books 10-50
7   Reid 5
8   *Dictionary of Welsh Biography* 386
9   Jones, E 1890 54
10 *Dictionary of Welsh Biography* 386
11 *ibid* 657
12 *ibid* 648
13 Jones, E. 1890 54
14 *Y Bywgraffiadur Cymreig 1941-50*   53

PASTIMES AND RECREATION

1.   Owen, George 1994 204-8, 298-300
2.   *ibid* 208-19, 300-3
3.   *Folklore* 1897 175
4.   Lewis, D. M. 126

EDUCATION

1.   Lewis, D M 204
2.   *Report ... on State of Education* 1847.

THE LAST 200 YEARS

1   Howell, R. L. 389
2   Stuart Jones, E H 85 passim
3   Kinross, J S 22
4   Evans, J J 178, 189
5   *Bulletin of the Board of Celtic Studies* xiv 147
6   *ibid* 151
7   Jones, F 1979 50-2
8   *Carmarthen Journal* 30 September 1811
9   Malkin, B. 449
10   Fenton 1811 544
11   Gastineau *sub* 'Newport'
12   Lewis, S II 267-8
13   Soulsby 48
14   Williams, D 155-6
15   *ibid* 267
16   *Cardigan and Tivy Side Advertiser* 27 April 1951
17   *County Echo* 15 February 1906
18   *ibid* 1 February 1906
19   *ibid* 11 November 1920
20   *ibid* 2 December 1920
21   *ibid* 27 September 1923
22   *ibid* 10 July 1958
23   *Arch Camb* 1970 125
24   Dyfed Archaeological Trust Report 1991-92
25   Miles 1993 197ff
26   Jones, E. 1890 40
27   *Newport, Pembrokeshire: Official Guide* 1916
28   Miles 1987 13ff

BIBLIOGRAPHY

BAKER, E.	'A Medieval Painting in Llanynys Church' in *Arch Camb* 1969
BALLINGER, J.	*Gleanings From a Printer's File*, Aberystwyth, 1928.
BARKER, C. T.	*The Chambered Tombs of South West-Wales*, Oxford, 1992.
BARONIA DE KEMEYS	*Arch Camb* Supplement. London, 1862.
BASSETT, D. A. & M. G. (ed)	*Geological Excursions in South Wales and the Forest of Dean*, Cardiff, 1971.
BEAUMONT, G. F.	*The Story of Combe Martin*, Combe Martin, 1959.
BENNETT, T.	*Welsh Shipwrecks* I, Haverfordwest, 1981.
BERESFORD, M.	*New Towns of the Middle Ages*, London, 1967.
BROWNE, D. M. *et al*	*An Architectural Study: Newport Castle (Pembrokeshire)*, Aberystwyth, 1992.
CAMDEN,Wm.	*Britannia*, ed. E. Gibson, London, 1722.
CHARLES, B. G.	*Calendar of the Records of the Borough of Haverfordwest, 1539-1660*. Cardiff, 1967.
CHARLES, B. G.	*George Owen of Henllys: A Welsh Elizabethan*. Aberystwyth, 1973.
CHARLES, B. G.	*The Place-names of Pembrokeshire* I & II, Aberystwyth,1992.
CHARLES, B. G.	'The Records of the Borough of Newport in Pembrokeshire' in the *National Library of Wales Journal*, VII, 1 and 2 (1951) 33 - 45, 120 - 137.
CHARLES, B. G.	'The Vicarage and Tithes of Nevern in Pembrokeshire' in *Journal of the Historical Society of the Church in Wales* I, 2 (1947), 26-39.
DAVIES, D.	*Those Were The Days* 2, Cardigan, 1992.
DAVIES, J. C. (ed)	*Episcopal Acts. . . relating to Welsh Dioceses 1066-1272*, I, Cardiff, 1946, 137, 242.
DAVIES, R. R.	*The Age of Conquest:Wales 1063-1415*, Oxford, 1991.
DAVIES, W.	*A General View of the Agriculture and Domestic Economy of South Wales*, 1815.
DWNN, Lewys	*Heraldic Visitations of Wales*, Llandovery, 1846.
ELLIS-GRUFFYDD, D.	*Rocks and Landforms in the Pembrokeshire Coast National Park*, 1, Newport, Pembs, 1977.
ELLIS-GRUFFYDD, D.	*Coastal Scenery of the Pembrokeshire Coast National Park*, 2, Newport, Pembs., 1977.

EVANS, E. J.   'Noddwyr y Beirdd yn Sir Benfro' in *Transactions of the Honourable Society of Cymmrodorion*, London, 1974.

EVANS, Gwynfor   *Land of My Fathers*, Swansea, 1974.

EVANS, J. J.   *Dylanwad y Chwyldro Ffrengig ar Lenyddiaeth Cymru*, Lerpwl 1928.

EVANS, J. T.   *The Church Plate of Pembrokeshire*. London, 1905.

FENTON, R.   'An Account of an Ancient Game...' in *The Cambrian Register for the Year 1795*, London, 1796.

FENTON, R.   'A History of Pembrokeshire' in *The Cambrian Register for the Year 1796*, London, 1799.

FENTON, R.   *A Historical Tour Through Pembrokeshire*, London, 1811.

GASTINEAU, H.   *Wales Illustrated in a Series of Views*, London, 1830.

GEORGE, T. N.   *British Regional Geology: South Wales*, London, 1970.

GERALD OF WALES   *The Journey Through Wales and the Description of Wales*, ed. L. Thorpe, London, 1978.

GODDARD, T.   *Pembrokeshire Shipwrecks*, Llandybie, 1983.

GREEN, F.
& BARKER, T.   'Pembrokeshire Parsons' in *West Wales Historical Records* III, Carmarthen, 1913.

GREENWAY, W.   'The Election of David Martin, Bishop of St. Davids 1293-6' in *Journal of the Historical Society of the Church in Wales* X, No 15 (1960), 9 - 16.

GREGORY, D.   *Country Churchyards in Wales*, Llanrwst, 1991.

GRIFFITHS, R. A.   *The Principality of Wales in the Later Middle Ages: South Wales 1277-1536*, Cardiff, 1972.

GRONO-BOOKS   *Two Hawkesbury Sailors*, Richmond, NSW, 1984.

GRUFFYDD, R. G.   'A Poem in Praise of Cuhelyn Fardd from the Black Book of Carmarthen',in *Studia Celtica* X/XI (1975-76), 198-209.

GUEST,
Lady Charlotte   *The Mabinogion*, London, 1906.

HOGG, A. H. A.   'Gaer Fawr and Carn Ingli: Two Major Pembrokeshire Hill-Forts' in *Arch Camb* CXXII, 1973.

HOGG, A. H. A. &
KING, D. J. C.   'Early Castles in Wales and the Marches' in *Arch Camb* CXII, 1 963.

HOGG, A. H. A. &
KING, D. J. C.   'Masonry Castles in Wales and the Marches' in *Arch Camb* CXVI, 1967.

HOLLAND, R.   *Basilikon Doron by King James I*, London, 1931.
HOWELL, J.   *Blodau Dyfed.* Carmarthen, 1824.
HOWELL, R. L.   'Pembrokeshire in Wartime' in *Pembrokeshire County History* III, 1987.
HOWELLS,
B. E. & N. A. (ed)   *The Extent of Cemais 1594*, Haverfordwest, 1977.
HOWELLS, B. E. (ed)   *Pembrokeshire County History III*, 1987.
HOWELLS, D. W.   *Patriarchs and Parasites*, Cardiff, 1986.
HOWELLS, D. W.   'Society 1660-1793'in *Pembrokeshire County History* III, 1987.
HOWELLS, D. W. (ed) *Pembrokeshire County History IV*, 1993
I'ANSON   *The History of the Martyn or Martin Families I*, London, 1935.
JENKINS, D. I. (ed)   *Looking Around Newport*, Cardigan, 1970.
JENKINS, J. G.   *Nets and Coracles*, Newton Abbot, 1974.
JENKINS, J. G.   *Maritime Heritage*, Llandysul, 1982.
JOHN, B.   *Pembrokeshire*, Newton Abbot, 1976.
JONES, D.   *Hanes y Bedyddwyr yn Nheheubarth Cymru*, Caerfyrddin, 1839,
JONES, E.   *A Historical Sketch of Newport Pembrokeshire*, Cardigan, 1890.
JONES, E.   *Deugain Mlynedd o'm Gweinidogaeth*, Caerfyrddin, 1894.
JONES, F.   *The Holy Wells of Wales*, Cardiff, 1954.
JONES, F.   'Bowen of Pentre Ifan and Llwyngwair' in *The Pembrokeshire Historian* No. 6, 1979.
JONES, F.   'Lloyd of Hendre and Cwmgloyn' in *National Library of Wales Journal* XXII 4, 1984.
JONES, G. &
JONES, T.   *The Mabinogion*, London, 1949.
JONES, T. T.   'Saint David' in *National Library of Wales Journal* XX 3, 1978.
KILMINSTER, G.
& MYTUM,H.   'Mariners at Newport, Pembrokeshire: Evidence from Gravestones' in *Cymru a'r Môr/Maritime Wales*, No 11, 1987.
KING, D. J. C.   'The Old Earldom of Pembroke' in *The Pembrokeshire Historian*, 7, 1981.
KING, D. J. C.   *Castellarium Anglicanum*, London, 1983.
KING, D. J. C.
& PERKS, J. C.   Newport Castle, 1949, unpubl. MSS. *penes me.*

KING, D. J. C.
& PERKS, J. C.   'Castell Nanhyfer, Nevern (Pembs)' in *Arch Camb* CI, 1951 .
KINROSS, J.C.   *Fishguard Fiasco.*, Tenby, 1974.
LELAND, J.   *The Itinerary in Wales in or about the years 1536-39*, ed. L. Toulin Smith, London, 1906.

LEWIS, D. M.   *Cofaint Evan Lewis. Brynberian*, Aberystwyth, 1903.

LEWIS, E. A. (ed)   *The Welsh Port Books (1550-1603)*, London, 1927.

LEWIS, S.   *A Topographical Dictionary of Wales*, London, 1848.

LLOYD, D. & M. (ed)   *A Book of Wales*, London, 1953.

LLOYD, E. J.   *Llafurwyr Seion*, Merthyr Tydfil, 1917.

LLOYD, H. A.   *The Gentry of South West-Wales. 1540-1640*, Cardiff, 1968.

LLOYD, J. E.   *A History of Wales from the Earliest times to the Edwardian Conquest*, London, 1912.

LLOYD, Lady K. H.   *An Epitome of the Twenty-five Lords of Kemes*, Carmarthen, 1930.

LLOYD, Thomas.   *The Lost Houses of Wales*, London, 1986.

LOCKLEY, R. M.   *Pembrokeshire*, London, 1957.

LYTE,
Sir H. C. Maxwell   'Burci, Falaise and Martin' in *Proceedings of the Somerset Archaeology and Natural Society*, 1919.

MACKIE, J. D.   *The Oxford History of England: The Early Tudors*, Oxford, 1957.

McKISACK, M.   *The Oxford History of England: The Fourteenth Century*, Oxford, 1959.

McNAB, R.   *Murihiku*, Invercargill, NZ. 1907.

MALKIN, B. H.   *The Scenery. Antiquities. and Biography of South Wales*, London, 1804.

MILES, Dillwyn (ed).   *Pembrokeshire Coast National Park*, HMSO, 1973.

MILES, Dillwyn,   *The Sheriffs of the County of Pembroke*, Haverfordwest, 1976.

MILES, Dillwyn,   *Portrait of Pembrokeshire*, London, 1984.

MILES, Dillwyn,   *The Pembrokeshire Coast National Park*, Newton Abbot, 1987.

MILES, Dillwyn,   'The Tourist Industry' in *Pembrokeshire County History. IV*, 1993.

MORGAN, P. B.   'Bronwydd and Sir Thomas Lloyd' in the *National Library of Wales Journal* XXIII 4, 1984.

MORRIS, L.   *Celtic Remains*, London, 1878.

MORRIS, L.   *Plans, Harbours, Bars, Bays and Roads in St. George's Channel*, London, 1748.

NASH-WILLIAMS
V. E.   *The Early Christian Monuments of Wales*, Cardiff, 1950.

OWEN, G. D.   *Elizabethan Wales*, Cardiff, 1964.

OWEN, George   *The Description of Penbrokshire* ed. Henry Owen, I (1892), II (1897), III (1906), IV (1936), London.

OWEN, George   *The Description of Pembrokeshire,* ed. Dillwyn Miles, Llandysul, 1994.

OWEN, George   *The Taylors Cussion,* ed. Emily Pritchard, London, 1906.

OWEN, H. (ed)   *Calendar of Public Records Relating to Pembrokeshire,* I (1911), II (1914), III (1918), London.

PHILLIPS, James.   *The History of Pembrokeshire,* London, 1909.

POWICKE, Sir, M.   *The Oxford History of England: The Thirteenth Century,* Oxford, 1962.

PRITCHARD, E. M.   *The History of St. Dogmael's Abbey,* London, 1907.

RADFORD, C. A.
Ralegh   *St. Dogmael's Abbey,* HMSO, 1962.

REES, Sian   *A Guide to Ancient and Historic Wales: Dyfed,* HMSO, 1992.

REES AND THOMAS *Hanes Eglwysi Annibynol Cymru* V, Dolgellau, 1891.

REEVES, A. C.   *The Marcher Lords,* Llandybie, 1983.

REID, G. R. S.   *The History of Ebenezer,* Windsor, NSW, 1940.

RICHARDS, G.   'Y Plygain' in *Journal of the Historical Society of Church in Wales* I, No. 2 (1947), 53-71.

RICHARDS, Lloyd   'Departed Glory' in *Newport Pem. Regatta Almanack and Year Book,* 1958.

ROBERTS, G. M.   *Y Pêr Ganiedydd,* I (1949) and II (1958), Caerdydd.

ROUND, J. H.   *Family Origins and other Studies,* London, 1930.

ROUND, J. H.   *The King's Serjeants and their Coronation Services,* London, 1911 .

SALMON, D.   'The Quakers of Pembrokeshire' in *West Wales Historical Records* IX, Carmarthen, 1923.

SAUNDERS, E.   *A View of the State of Religion in the Diocese of St. David's,* 1721.

SIDDONS, M. P.   *The Development of Welsh Heraldry,* I (1991), II & III (1993), Aberystwyth.

SOULSBY, L.   *The Towns of Medieval Wales,* Chichester, 1983.

STEPHENS, M. (ed). *The Oxford Companion to the Literature of Wales,* Oxford, 1986.

STUART JONES,
E. H.   *The Last Invasion of Britain,* Cardiff, 1950.

THOMAS, P.   *Strangers from a Secret Land,* Llandysul, 1986.

THORNE, R.   'Pembrokeshire and National Politics' in *Pembrokeshire County History* IV, 1993.

THORNE, R. (ed).   *The History of Parliament 1790-1820,* London.

TUCKER, M.   'Facts about Tides' in *Newport (Pem.) Regatta Almanack and Year Book* 1958.

TURVEY, R.   'Nevern Castle: A New Interpretation' in *The Journal of the Pembrokeshire Historical Society* 3 (1989) 57, 60.

VAUGHAN, H. M.   *The South Wales Squires,* London, 1926.

VINCENT, H. J.   'Caerau in St. Dogmaels' in *Arch. Camb,* 1864.
WADE-EVANS, A. W.   *Vitae Sanctorum Britanniae et Genealogie,*
                        Cardiff, 1944.
WAINWRIGHT,C. J.   *A Guide to the Pembrokeshire Coast Path,*
                        London, 1986.
WALLACE-HADRILL,
F. E.   *The Parish Church of St. Mary. Newport,*
                        Pembrokeshire, Cardigan, 1989.
WILLIAMS, A. H. (ed)   *John Wesley in Wales.* Cardiff, 1971.
WILLIAMS, David.   *The Rebecca Riots,* Cardiff, 1955.
WYNDHAM, H. P.   *A Gentleman's Tour Through Monmouthshire and*
                        Wales., 1774, London, 1775.

Archaeologia Cambrensis.
Bronwydd Collection of Manuscripts and Records, National Library of
Wales.
The Dictionary of Welsh Biography down to 1940, London, 1959.
Y Bywgraffiadur Cymreig 1941-1950, London, 1970.
Dyfed Archaeological Trust Report on Projects, 1991-92.
Inventory of Ancient Monuments in Wales and Monmouthshire: County of
Pembroke, HMS0, 1925.
Law Commission Report: Jurisdiction of Certain Ancient Courts, HMS0,
1976.
Report of the Commissioners of Enquiry into the State of Education in Wales
under R R W Lingen, HMS0, 1847.
Report of the Municipal Corporation Commission, HMSO, 1835.
Pigot's Directory 1830.
Slater's Directory: South Wales 1880.
Penbont Bridge Committee Minutes 1891-94.

INDEX

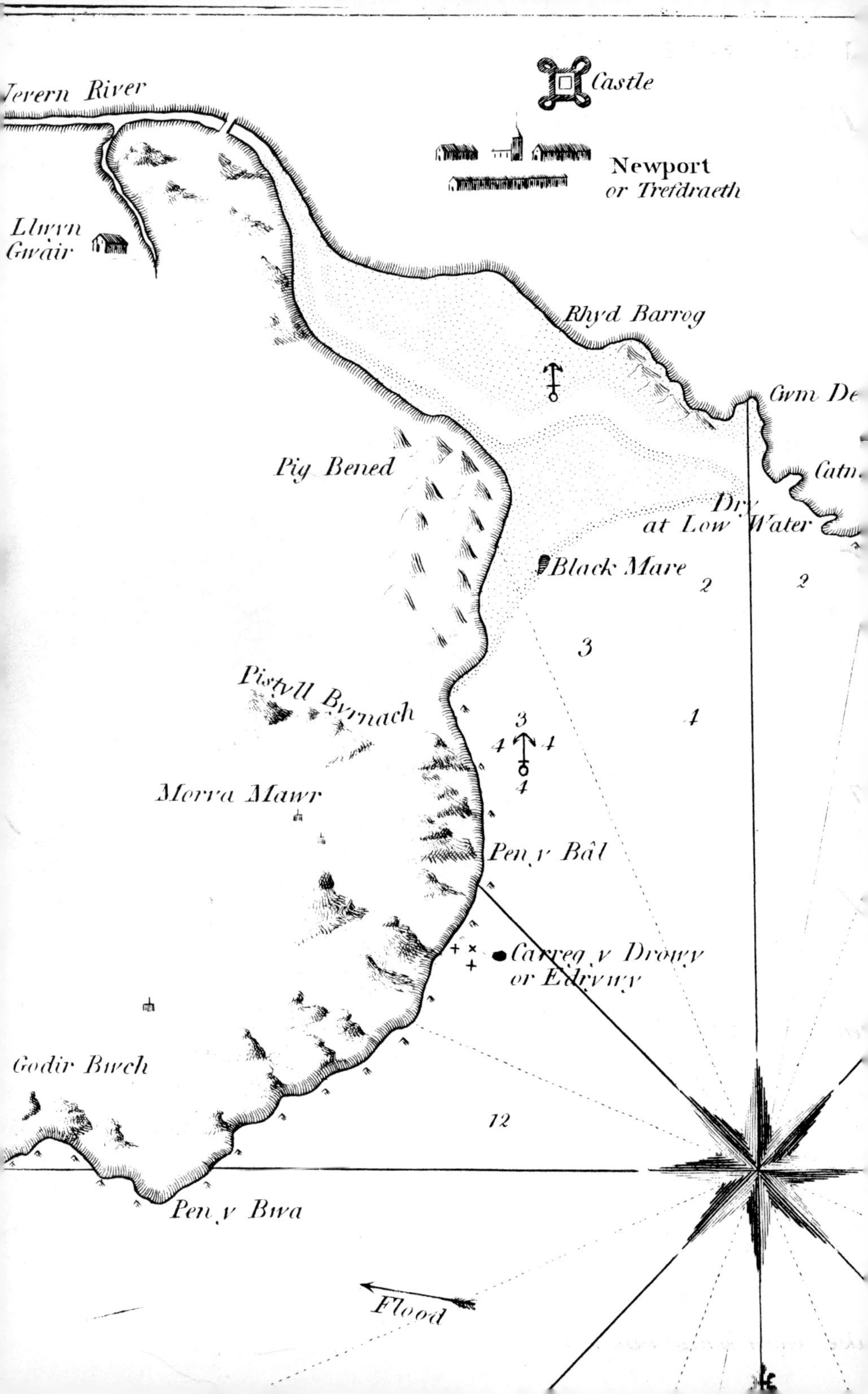

Severn River

Castle

Newport
or Trefdraeth

Llwyn
Gwair

Rhyd Barrog

Pig Bened

Gwm De

Catn

Dry
at Low Water

Black Mare   2   2

3

Pistull Byrnach   4   3   4   4
                              ○
                              4

Morva Mawr

Pen y Bâl

Carreg y Drowy
or Edrywy

Godir Bwch

12

Pen y Bwa

Flood